Lecture Notes in Computer Science

Lecture Notes in Computer Science

Edited by G. Goos and J. Hartmanis

238

Lee Naish

Negation and Control in Prolog

Springer-Verlag
Berlin Heidelberg New York London Paris Tokyo

Author

Lee Naish
Computer Science Department, University of Melbourne
Parkville 3052, Australia

CR Subject Classifications (1985): I.2.3, D.3.2, H.3.4

ISBN 3-540-16815-X Springer-Verlag Berlin Heidelberg New York
ISBN 0-387-16815-X Springer-Verlag New York Berlin Heidelberg

Library of Congress Cataloging-in-Publication Data. Naish, Lee, 1960- Negation and control in
PROLOG. (Lecture notes in computer science; 238) Bibliography: p. 1. Prolog (Computer program
language) I. Title. II. Series.
QA76.73.P76N35 1986 005.13'3 86-22056
ISBN 0-387-16815-X (U.S.)

© Springer-Verlag Berlin Heidelberg 1986
Printed in Germany

Printing and binding: Druckhaus Beltz, Hemsbach/Bergstr.
2145/3140-543210

ABSTRACT

We investigate ways of bringing PROLOG closer to the ideals of logic programming, by improving its facilities for negation and control. The forms of negation available in conventional PROLOG systems are implemented unsoundly, and can lead to incorrect solutions. We discuss several ways in which negation as failure can be implemented soundly. The main forms of negation considered are *not, not-equals, if-then-else* and all solutions predicates. The specification and implementation of all solutions predicates is examined in detail. Allowing quantifiers in negated calls is an extension which is easily implemented and we stress its desirability, for all forms of negation. We propose other enhancements to current implementations, to prevent the computation aborting or looping infinitely, and also outline a new technique for implementing negation by program transformation. Finally, we suggest what forms of negation should be implemented in future PROLOG systems.

The poor control facilities of conventional PROLOG lead to infinite loops and inefficiency. More flexible computation rules can often overcome these problems. We first introduce control primitives for database and recursive predicates, then show how control information can be generated automatically, using these primitives. Automatically reordering subgoals in clauses is also considered. This allows programmers to concentrate more on the logic of a problem, making programming simpler. We give examples using several different styles of programming. The implications of automatic control for the design of control primitives is also discussed.

Next, we re-examine the theoretical foundations of PROLOG systems with flexible computation rules. The SLD resolution model is extended, to correct a previous over-simplification. The extension also brings to light a much greater flexibility of computation rules, which has previously been overlooked. A rule which behaves like intelligent backtracking is given as an example. Finally, we take an overview of the many approaches to control in PROLOG. Some general principles for evaluating and classifying control rules are given. These show the deficiencies of current systems more clearly. We make suggestions for future implementations of PROLOG with extra control facilities.

PREFACE

This book is essentially the same as my Ph.D. thesis, with some minor corrections. The research presented here was done in conjunction with the development of the MU-Prolog system. Since then the successor to MU-Prolog, called NU-Prolog [MIP 86], has been implemented. It has different control facilities, mentioned here briefly, and more advanced negation facilities, based on this work, [Naish 86a], and [Lloyd 84a]. Further work on the database system has also been fruitful [Ramamohanarao 86], [Thom 86], [Naish 86b], [Balbin 86].

Lee Naish

PREFACE TO THESIS

The basic thrust of the work presented here is towards improving PROLOG, so it is closer to the ideal of logic programming. It should be possible to write programs declaratively, using simple logic, and have them executed efficiently. One positive result we have had is in the development of the MU-PROLOG system [Naish 82] [Naish 85a]. It is used quite widely as a general purpose PROLOG system. The distributed version now also includes a database system, mainly implemented by James Thom [Naish 83b]. An improved version, implemented by John Shepherd and Kotagiri Ramamohanarao, will be released soon. We do not discuss the system much in the body of this thesis, but a technical report on the database system and the MU-PROLOG Reference Manual appear as appendices.

The two main problems with PROLOG, as a logic programming language, are the unsound implementation of negation, and the poor control facilities. Unsound negation can cause incorrect answers, and poor control leads to inefficient computations and infinite loops. Both problems are a result of the fixed, left to right, computation rule. This thesis examines how more flexible computation rules can be used to improve negation and control in PROLOG.

Part I deals with implementing sound forms of negation. Previous implementations are reviewed and several new ideas are added. In particular, the area of all solutions predicates is examined in detail. This section contains essentially the same material as [Naish 85c]. Other work in this chapter, on preventing aborting, avoiding infinite loops, and program transformation, etc, has not appeared elsewhere, to date.

Part II is divided into three main chapters, all dealing with control. The first, and largest, discusses how control can be automated. This is particularly important as a means to make programming easier. The main results appeared as [Naish 85b], but here we include some new enhancements, more examples and more discussion about recent related approaches to control. The second chapter re-examines the SLD resolution model of PROLOG systems with flexible computation rules. The model is generalised, correcting a previous oversight. This has appeared as [Naish 84a], though we include more discussion here. The final chapter takes an overview of the many approaches to control, and attempts to find some guiding principals for the design of future systems. It is based on [Naish 84c], a shorter version of which appeared as [Naish 85d].

ACKNOWLEDGEMENTS

I wish to acknowledge the support of all my friends during the time this work was done. In particular, John Lloyd introduced logic programming research to Melbourne University, supervised this research, commented on many drafts of my papers and thesis, and did some useful hacking of lpp. His enthusiasm was important in building a strong logic programming group in Melbourne. Other people who deserve my thanks for commenting on drafts of my papers include Rodney Topor, Jean-Louis Lassez, Jason Catlett (official proof reader), Maurice Bruynooghe and Alan Robinson. Jean-Louis Lassez also enriched the group considerably and the hours spent in his office were very profitable. Thanks also go to the other postgrads, including the non-logic programmers (may they see the light some day).

The computing environment was also important, for my implementation work on and in MU-PROLOG, and for text processing. Robert Elz must be thanked for his work on maintaining the system, improving our access to the network, and helping with some gross hacks to make MU-PROLOG do things which UNIX™ does not support. The logic programming bibliography, and associated software, collected by Isaac Balbin and Koenrad Lecot was of great use. Also, David Price's development of "term" made logging in a joy. Without the generous loan of a computer from Pyramid Technology, the early implementation work in the Machine Intelligence Project would not have been possible. My work has been supported by a grant to the Machine Intelligence Project and a CPRA.

Table of Contents

PART I – IMPLEMENTING NEGATION

1. IMPLEMENTING NEGATION AS FAILURE

1.1. Introduction

It is not possible to express negative information with pure Horn clauses. They state what is true but not what is false. Negation is obviously an important aspect of logic programming languages, and good implementations should be available. In this thesis we just deal with the implementation of the negation as failure rule [Clark 78]. Because of the restricted nature of this form of negation, and the criticism there has been of it, we feel this needs some justification.

There are several ways negation can be added to Horn clauses. In order of increasing complexity, we could allow negated atoms in the queries, the bodies of clauses or the heads of clauses. Negation in the heads of clauses gives us the full power of first order logic and, consequently, needs a more expensive form of resolution. The great advantage of Horn clauses, as a programming language, is that SLD resolution can be implemented very efficiently. It seems unlikely that more general forms of resolution can achieve this order of efficiency. Negation in the heads of clauses may have to be left to automatic theorem proving rather than logic programming.

Assuming the standard semantics of a clause being an implication, we cannot use a program to prove anything is false without negation in the heads of clauses. However, the negation as failure inference rule can be used: a goal is false if we can prove that it cannot be proved. It is a less powerful but implementable version of the closed world assumption [Reiter 78]: a goal is false if it cannot be proved. One major advantage of negation as failure is that it can be implemented with essentially no extra cost to the resolution system.

Some people have criticized negation as failure on the grounds that it is not "real" negation. Actually, negation as failure can be seen as ordinary negation, using the *completion* of the program [Clark 78]. This is found by combining all clauses of each predicate and forming *if and only if* definitions. We could consider that a program is a shorthand for its completion. If the semantics the programmer wants are the open world assumption (which is unusual), instead of the closed world assumption, this can be achieved by adding additional tautologies. In the example below, the second clause does not contribute anything to the if definition – nothing extra can be proved with it. However, it does affect the iff definition, so fewer things can be proved false. p(b) cannot be disproved, though it could without the second clause.

    p(a).
    p(X) :- p(X).

With the iff definition, positive literals are proved with resolution on the if part of the program, as before. Proving negative literals is equivalent to resolution using just the only if part of the completion. The two parts are not mixed, which explains why the search space of the refutation procedure remains small, compared to other resolution strategies.

Negation as failure can be used in queries and in clause bodies. In some work the distinction between these two cases has been played down or ignored. Just allowing negated atoms in the initial query is very useful for database applications, where programs tend to be simple and queries complex. However, for general programming, and deductive databases with numerous rules, negation in the program itself gives much more expressive power and is really what we need. An example of the the distinction being ignored is the negation based on intuitionistic logic discussed in [Sakai 83]. This form of negation applies only to single negated atoms in the query. It can be extended to multiple atoms fairly easily, but not to negated atoms in program clauses. The completeness of negation as failure [Jaffar 83] also relies on the absence of negation in the program. There are simple examples which show that negation as failure is not always complete if there are negations in the program. However, it seems that it is complete for most current programs.

So, although negation as failure is restricted, it has the advantage of being possible to implement it significantly more efficiently than more general forms of negation. It has also served the logic programming community reasonably well to date and is very unlikely to be superseded in the foreseeable future. However, the implementation of negation as failure still needs improvement. The most common version is actually unsound. We therefore address the task of implementing negation as failure (NAF) in clause bodies. We also examine the very closely related area of finding all solutions to a query.

In the rest of this chapter, we review the work of others, and present some new analysis and ideas of our own. We first examine several unsoundly implemented forms of negation, available in some PROLOG systems. The non-logical behaviour of some of these primitives has been overlooked by many people in the past. Next, we introduce a version of *not* which delays until it is ground. This idea is not new, but we discuss some of its limitations more than previous work. We then describe how the implementation can be extended, to allow universal quantifiers. MU-PROLOG is the only system we know of that supports this simple, but important, idea. IC-PROLOG's *not* is then described, and its limitations are also discussed. We suggest several new ways in which it can be enhanced. We first show how to prevent it aborting, then investigate ways to avoid infinite loops. Inequality is discussed next. Again, universal quantifiers have been ignored in other implementations.

The next section deals with all solutions predicates, and is our largest contribution in this chapter. We show how all previous implementations can behave non-logically, and how the previous specification cannot be implemented efficiently. A new specification is given, along with an implementation which uses a sound inequality predicate, with universal quantifiers. The main ideas behind the next two section, on negative unifiers and program transformation, have been discovered independently several times. We presented the ideas in 1984†. Papers on them have subsequently appeared, so we keep our discussion brief. However, we do present a new way that program transformation can be used for implementing negation, based on functions. We conclude with our

---

† Workshop on Fifth Generation Languages, University of Melbourne, January 1984.

opinion of what facilities for negation should be implemented in future PROLOG systems.

1.2. Unsound Implementations

Here we discuss several of the unsoundly implemented forms of negation available in some PROLOG systems. Answers can be returned which are not logical consequences of the program. Avoiding incorrect answers requires that the programmer have detailed knowledge of the operational, as well as declarative, semantics of programs. Logic programming aims to avoid this.

1.2.1. Not and Not Equals

By far the most common version of *not* (or \+) available in PROLOG systems can be implemented as follows.

    not(G) :- call(G), !, fail.
    not(G).

Inequality can be implemented using *not*, but is normally implemented as a special case, as follows.

    X \= X :- !, fail.
    X \= Y.

If not(G) is called and the call to G fails, then not(G) succeeds. This is correct by the NAF rule. If the call to G succeeds, cut and fail are called so not(G) fails. This is not part of the NAF rule and can cause incorrect behaviour if G contains variables. For example,

$$\leftarrow not(X=1), X=2.$$

This goal fails (incorrectly) if *not* is called first, but succeeds if it is called after X has been bound. The desired semantics of not(X=1) is $\exists X \neg X=1$. Instead, $\exists X \ X=1$ is computed and the result is negated, giving $\neg\exists X \ X=1$ or $\forall X \ \neg X=1$. Sometimes, the negated goal can be proved without binding any variables in the call. With the goal not(X=X), for example, we prove $\forall X \ X=X$. Negated, this is $\neg\exists X \ \neg X=X$, so *not* correctly fails. The case that causes unsoundness therefore, is when there are solutions to the negated goal, but all of them cause variables in the goal to be bound. No proof can be found where all variables are universally quantified so there is no logical justification for *not* failing. Another way of looking at it is that it is impossible to determine whether *not* should succeed or fail until the call is more instantiated.

If this form of negation is used, a great deal of care must be taken to ensure it is called only when certain variables have been bound. With the conventional PROLOG computation rule, this can often be done by reordering subgoals in the program. However, this may result in *not* being called later than is desirable, resulting in inefficiency. With more complex computation rules, avoiding unsafe calls to this form of *not* is more difficult. Forms of *not* that ensure correct behaviour are desirable.

1.2.2. If Then Else

Not can be generalised to an if-then-else predicate as follows:

    if C then A else B :- C, !, A.
    if C then A else B :- B.

The meaning of "if C then A else B" (in DEC-10 PROLOG, this is written C -> A ; B) is intended to be (C ∧ A) ∨ (¬C ∧ B). The *else* part is normally optional – "if C then A" (or C –> A) means (C ∧ A) ∨ (¬C). The cut primitive is often used for implementing these semantics, without executing the test twice. Using *if-then-else* instead makes declarative reading of programs much easier. However, it can behave unsoundly in exactly the same way as *not*. If the test succeeds but binds variables, incorrect answers can result. Because of the unsound negation, (¬C ∧ B) is not implemented correctly. Also, since only the first solution of C is considered, (C ∧ A) is not implemented correctly either.

1.2.3. Soft Cut and Cases

Soft cut is a variant of cut which removes fewer choice points. Consider the previous *if-then-else* definition, with cut replaced by soft cut. Calling soft cut prevents backtracking to the second clause, but does not remove choice points from the execution of C. In other words, the test may backtrack and produce more solutions. This is the basis of the *cases* construct in LM-PROLOG and some versions of C-PROLOG. For *if-then-else*, (C ∧ A) is implemented correctly but (¬C ∧ B) still has the same trouble. It should probably be considered a small improvement on the more traditional form.

1.2.4. All Solutions Predicates

All solutions predicates provide a way of collecting all solutions to a goal. Negation can be implemented by checking if the number of solutions is zero. Because of the complexity of this topic, we will leave all the details until our complete discussion in Section 1.9. Very briefly, we show how a logical all solutions predicate can be implemented and used for negation, though all previous implementations can behave non-logically.

1.2.5. Epilog and Two Level PROLOG

Epilog [Porto 82] and Two Level PROLOG [Porto 84] are extensions of PROLOG, with extra facilities for control and negation. Unfortunately, the negation is implemented by a naive translation back into PROLOG, with cuts. The implementation is unsound, but it is hidden more from the user. We consider this a dangerous move. Developing higher level logic programming languages than PROLOG is desirable, but they should be built on sound foundations. It is difficult enough to debug a PROLOG program with an error due to unsound negation. Epilog and Two Level PROLOG encourage the use of negation more, but debugging is made more difficult.

1.3. Delaying Until Ground

The simplest way to make the implementation of *not* sound, is to delay all calls to it until they are ground [Dahl 80]. This is done with MU-PROLOG's ~ predicate and has been shown to be sound [Clark 78]. Similarly, MU-PROLOG's *if-then-else* delays until the test is ground. Delaying makes ordering the subgoals easier. An attempt to call *not* can be made as early as is convenient (or efficient), and the call will be delayed until it is safe. In database applications, where data structures and procedures are simple, this form of *not* usually suffices. Negated calls rarely succeed without binding any variables before they are ground, so calling *not* earlier would gain nothing. However, with recursive data structures and procedures, this is not the case. Consider the following example.

```
member(A, A.B).
member(A, B.C) :- member(A, C).

    ← not member(1, [1,X]).
```

The call to *member* would succeed without constructing X, so *not* could fail, but it actually delays. *Not* will only fail when X eventually becomes ground. This type of behaviour often increases the time complexity of programs operating on recursive data structures, and can even cause infinite loops. *Member* is probably the most commonly negated predicate, at least when using recursive data structures, and its behaviour is typical. We use it for many examples.

1.3.1. Universal Quantifiers

There is a simple extension of this form of negation which allows goals with some variables universally quantified, for example, $\forall X \neg p(X,Y)$. We simply delay until all existentially quantified variables are ground. We must also ensure that the universally quantified variables are not bound at the time of the call. The best way to do this it to ensure that they only appear in the call to *not*. This implementation of *not* works the same way as the unsound version, except we can control which variables are (effectively) existentially and universally quantified. It is available as a MU-PROLOG library predicate and has proved very useful, especially in database queries and the implementation of Extended PROLOG [Lloyd 84a]. For example, suppose we have a database with a relation listing all employees, and a relation listing their offices. If we wanted to find the employees who are not allocated offices, it would be expressed as follows.

```
    ← employee(E), forall(O, not(office(E, O))).
```

With Extended PROLOG, the *forall* construct would be translated into a call to *gnot*. *Gnot* would just wait until E is ground, then proceed as not(office(E,O)) normally would. Because this version of *not* must wait for the (implicitly) existentially quantified variables, rather than the (explicitly) universally quantified variables, it is most efficient to translate the call at compile time. In the translated call, the existentially quantified variables are made explicit. In the example above, we get gnot(E, office(E,O)). This saves analysing the call at run time.

1.4. IC-PROLOG Not

IC-PROLOG's *not* predicate [Clark 79] can sometimes avoid the inefficiency caused by *not* delaying when it could fail. IC-PROLOG *not* does not delay, but attempts to find a proof of the goal without binding any variables in the call. If such a proof is found, *not* fails. If the negated goal has no solutions then *not* succeeds. Otherwise (there are solutions but they bind variables), *not* aborts with a control error. Unless the program is carefully written, so *not* is never called too soon, this last case is unfortunately common. The better performance in the previous *member* example cannot often be used, because in cases such as the following, the computation is aborted.

```
    ← not member(1, [2,X]).
```

Calling *not* too soon can also result in the negated goal having an infinite number of solutions. This causes non-terminating search for a proof which binds no variables in the call. One possibility is to use the IC-PROLOG form of *not* only to enhance the MU-PROLOG form slightly. The call normally delays until it is ground, but if it never becomes ground, the IC-PROLOG method is used.

1.4.1. Retrying Instead of Aborting

Another way we suggest for improving the behaviour of IC-PROLOG's *not*, is delay the call and retry it at a later stage, rather than aborting. If the call is retried often enough, we can ensure it will fail as soon as possible. The simplest method is to retry it whenever a variable in it is bound. This can result in great inefficiency, because of the number of times the goal is retried. Obviously we should attempt to minimize the number of retries, consistent with failing quickly. We discuss way this can be achieved in the next section. After that, we discuss ways to deal with infinite numbers of solutions.

1.4.1.1. Minimizing the Number of Retries

We want *not* to fail as quickly as possible, without retrying the call more than necessary. Making *not* succeed quickly is sometimes useful, but can also lead to greater inefficiency. If the rest of the computation is nondeterministic, then *not* is called fewer times if it succeeds quickly. If the negated call is nondeterministic, however, delaying further can speed up the execution of *not*. Also, the more *not* is retried, the more time will be wasted when it can neither succeed or fail. We therefore suggest only retrying *not* when one of the previous proofs may no longer bind any of the calls variables.

Some systems (MU-PROLOG, for example) allow a goal to be delayed until one of several variables are bound. The best use of this feature is to remember one variable which was bound for each proof of the negated goal, and wait for any of these variables to be bound. With luck, the proof(s) in which the newly bound variable was bound can then be duplicated, without binding any variables from the call, so *not* can fail. Note that other variables, that were not waited on, may have been bound first. These bindings could only have made *not* succeed.

It is possible to retry even less than this, if all the variables bound in each proof are remembered. We should wait until all variables that were bound in some proof are bound. This requires a more complicated criterion for waking the call but, when retrying is expensive, it is worth the effort.

By remembering the actual solutions to the negated goal, rather than just which variables are bound, retrying can be eliminated completely. When a variable in the call is bound, its binding can be compared with its bindings in all solutions to the goal. If the current bindings become incompatible with all the solutions, *not* can succeed. If the bindings become the same as those in one of the solutions, *not* can fail. This is discussed further, along with a proposed implementation, in the section on all solutions predicates.

1.4.1.2. Infinite Numbers of Solutions

Even if *not* is retried instead of being aborted when variables are bound, calling it too early can cause difficulties. If the negated call has an infinite number of solutions, all of which bind variables in the goal, the result is an infinite loop. A fruitless attempt is made to search the tree for a proof that binds no variables in the goal. Infinite loops are predominately a problem for the control of logic programs, and we will deal with them further in Part II. However, the particular case of negation has some unique features, and is of interest. Firstly, because the entire tree may have to be searched and the goal within *not* is separate from the rest of the computation, the tendency for infinite loops is increased. Secondly, it is possible to stop the computation prematurely, if it is retried later.

The first idea for a partial solution, is to delay negated goals until they have a finite number of solutions. Obviously, this criterion is very difficult to implement in practice, but we give some helpful heuristics in our work on automating control. It would be possible to extend these for negation. Even if this rule could be implemented exactly, the resulting form of negation would not be very good. Consider the following two goals.

← not member(1, 2.X).
← not member(1, 1.X).

The first goal should indeed delay. However, the second goal should fail, even though the call to member has an infinite number of solutions. Distinguishing between these two types of goals, without actually calling them, seems impossible.

An alternative is to do a (generally) incomplete search of the tree, only doing a complete search as a last resort. There are limitless possibilities for this and we will discuss a few. Probably the simplest is to put some depth limit on the tree. [Brough 84] suggest other similar methods which ensure a finite search, such as limiting the number of applications of each rule. The major difficulty of these methods is finding an appropriate limit. Some goals, such as *member*, may need large limits, whereas other goals may need small limits to avoid a combinatorial explosion. Even progressive deepening does not help much.

A different approach is to look at just the first N solutions to the goal (for some N). Ideally, the tree should be searched in a breadth first manner. This is rather inefficient in practice, so a combination of depth first search and intelligent clause ordering is more feasible. By placing recursive clauses last, it is usually fairly easy (though not always possible) to make successful derivations appear before infinite ones. When there are an infinite number of solutions, only the leftmost branch(es) are explored. Consider the previous definition of *member* (with the recursive rule last). The first solution to *member* in the goal ← not member(1,1.X) does not bind X, so *not* can fail. With the goal ← not member(1,X.1.Y), the first two solutions are needed if the goal is to fail.

It is possible to explore more of the tree, with little chance of infinite loops or a combinatorial explosion, by modifying the naive backtracking algorithm. When a solution is found, it is best to backtrack to the first call that bound a variable in the negated goal (if no such call exists, *not* fails). It is pointless backtracking any less than this, since any extra solutions must have bound a variable in the goal. With a breadth first search, or appropriate clause ordering, this method is quite effective at making the search finite, whilst maintaining completeness with respect to solutions that bind no variables in the goal. Infinite loops result if there is an infinite subtree with no success branches, or an infinite branch from the root with no goal variable binding. The second case implies there is a ground instance of the goal with an infinite SLD tree. Both these cases occur only with pathological programs that are relatively rare. Consider the following program and goal.

member2(A, B, C) :− member(A, B), member(A, C).

← not member2(1, X.1.Y, 1.Z).

The first solution binds X to 1. With normal backtracking, the second call to *member* would be retried. With our method, we would backtrack to the first call, avoiding the infinite number of alternative solutions to the second call. The solution which binds no variables is then found, so the goal can fail. The goal below also leads to a short computation.

← not member(1, X).

Two solutions to *member* are found (X=1.B and X=B.1.B1), then backtracking forces *member* to fail. This shows that the call has solutions, but all of them bind X. *Not* must therefore be aborted, and retried when X is bound.

If the computation backtracks as soon as a variable in the goal is bound (rather than waiting for a solution to be found), the amount of computation is reduced. Occasionally, finite failure of the goal may not be detected, but this method has the significant advantage of not needing intelligent clause ordering. The previous two examples we gave would have resulted in infinite loops if the recursive rule for *member* was first. If backtracking takes place as soon as X is bound, this is avoided.

A final possibility comes from our work on control in Part II. It is possible to produce control information specifically to delay calls known to have an infinite number of solutions. The negated call could be run with this control. The tree would then not be searched beyond points where all subgoals are delayed. As in the last two schemes described, this results in more relevant parts of the tree being searched, without a combinatorial explosion. Intelligent clause ordering is not needed either. With the *member2* goal we gave, the second call to *member* delays when it is retried. Backtracking then proceeds to the first call, as before. In the other example, ← member(1,X) delays immediately.

1.5. Inequality

One simple type of goal for which negation can easily be implemented is equality. There can be no infinite loops and, because it is so simple, it can be retried efficiently. MU-PROLOG and PROLOG II both have soundly implemented inequality predicates. An important advantage of MU-PROLOG's ~=, is that it allows universal quantification to be expressed, by having underscores as variable names. The system ensures that each underscore in a clause denotes a unique variable. An example of its use is X ~= _._, which means $\forall Y,Z\ X \neq Y.Z$. This reasonably common case of checking that a variable is not bound to a cons cell, cannot be expressed without universal quantifiers. The following program, for "flattening" lists of lists, illustrates the need for it.

```
flatten([ ], [ ]).
flatten([ ].A, B) :- flatten(A,B).
flatten((A.B).C, D) :- flatten(A.B.C, D).
flatten(A.B, A.C) :- A ~= [ ], A ~= _._, flatten(B, C).
```

Using underscores to denote universally quantified variables is very concise and ensures the variables only occur within the call to ~=, but has two disadvantages. The first is that some inequalities cannot easily be expressed because all underscores denote distinct variables. For example, $\forall Y\ X{\neq}f(Y,Y)$ must be implemented as (X ~= f(_,_) ; X = f(Y,Z), Y ~= Z), rather than a single call to ~=. The other difficulty occurs in systems programming. Manipulating underscores and distinguishing them from other variables is difficult using the meta-logical facilities of current systems.

The current implementation of ~= is as follows. An attempt to unify the two arguments of the call is made. If this fails, the calls succeeds. If the unification succeeds without binding any non-underscore† variables, the call fails. Otherwise, the first non-underscore variable to be bound is marked and the call delays. When the marked variable is bound, the call is retried in the same way. This can be inefficient in some cases. Consider the following goal.

$$\leftarrow X1 \sim= [1,2,3,4,5,6], \ldots$$

If X1 is successively bound to 1.X2, 1.2.X3, and so on, the front of the list is unified many times. The time spent on all the calls to ~= can be $O(N^2)$, where N is the length of the list. This can be avoided, by saving the frontier where the terms may differ, and using this for the resumed calls. The frontier consists of the non-underscore variables that are bound, and the terms to which they are bound. With the previous example, this method would result in the following calls.

```
← X1 ~= [1,2,3,4,5,6].
← 1.X2 ~= [1,2,3,4,5,6].
← 2.X3 ~= [2,3,4,5,6].
← 3.X4 ~= [3,4,5,6].
    . . .
```

Each of these calls can be done in constant time, so the total time spent is proportional to the length of the list. We believe inequality with universal quantifiers has an important role to play in negation for logic programming, so this more efficient implementation is desirable.

1.6. Incremental Not

The idea of an implementation of *not* that proceeds incrementally, delaying each time it attempts to bind a variable in the call, is initially appealing. It is also a popular notion, which justifies some discussion of it, even though our conclusions are discouraging. The aim of delaying instead of constructing variables is to avoid the inefficiency of aborting and retrying. It also implies than *not* might not fail (or succeed) as quickly as it could, since it may delay after only part of the

---

† Only underscores appearing in the call to ~= are treated specially. Variables bound to other underscores are considered non-underscores (this is implemented by checking the environment pointer).

SLD tree is examined. In fact, just searching for the first solution to the negated goal is superior in this regard. However, the main objections concern the complexity of implementation.

Initially, let us consider the simplest case: a single call to *not* within a larger goal. We shall refer to the execution of the negated goal as the *inner* computation and the rest as the *outer* computation. Generally, the execution involves some interleaving of the inner and outer computations. Whenever the inner computation attempts to (further) instantiate a variable from the initial call, it must be delayed. This can be detected by marking the variables and distinguishing between the two computations in some way. If the inner computation succeeds, the outer computation must backtrack, to the most recent choice point of the outer computation. This entails backtracking over some or all of the inner computation and ignoring choice points there.

If the inner computation reaches a point where it fails, and must backtrack, things are more complicated. Firstly, the backtracking must not affect the outer computation in any way. Secondly, the outer computation may subsequently backtrack, which must result in the inner computation "unbacktracking", to restore its previous state. In essence, this is the same as retrying part of the goal. It is safe to backtrack normally, discarding information, to the most recent part of the outer computation. Any further backtracking must not lose any information, since it may have to be undone. If we backtrack to the start of the inner computation, the outer computation is simply continued. *Not* succeeds but may still be backtracked into.

All this is obviously a headache for the implementor and probably results in significant overheads. Furthermore, this is just the beginning. In practice, there can be several concurrent calls to *not*, which must not interfere with each other, though their computations may be interleaved. Even worse, there can be calls to *not* from within calls to *not*. At this point we conclude that better forms of *not* can be implemented more easily.

1.7. All Solutions Predicates

1.7.1. Introduction

It is generally accepted by the PROLOG programming community, that an "all solutions" predicate is a useful extension to the language. As well as being able to express negation, it is very valuable in its own right. This work is intended to clear up some of the confusion which has arisen due to the ad hoc development of many such predicates. [Clark 80] have developed a specification for one predicate but it cannot be implemented efficiently. There are also many implementations but they can all behave non-logically, for a variety of reasons, including the unsound implementation of inequality. To illustrate this, we show how the *var* predicate can be implemented. Unlike [Kahn 84], we consider this non-logical behaviour to be a bug, rather than a feature. It implies that the behaviour of these "predicates" cannot be described in a declarative way.

We begin by summarising previous work and illustrating its shortcomings. The realisation that current implementations have faults is not new, and some failings have been briefly discussed in the literature (for example, [Kahn 84]). Here a more detailed and comprehensive account is given and a solution is proposed. We adapt Clark's specification, then show how this can be implemented, using a sound implementation of a form of inequality. The result is comparable in efficiency with current implementations and has the major advantage that it has a well defined declarative semantics. Because of this, it can be used for an interesting implementation of negation.

1.7.2. Background

In this section we summarize the work which has been done on specification of all solutions predicates and outline several implementations (with various names). We will use the name *solutions* when referring to the predicates in general and the particular version we develop.

1.7.2.1. Specification

In [Clark 80], the following specification appears (using slightly different notation):

solutions(T, G, S) $\longleftrightarrow$
$\forall X(\exists L_1,..,L_n(G \wedge X=T) \longleftrightarrow$ member(X, S))

G is a PROLOG goal and S is a list, containing an instance of term T for each solution to G. $L_1,..,L_n$ is the list of local variables in G. The distinction between local and global variables is an important one. It affects the semantics and is one reason why some implementations behave non-logically. The convention we shall use is that variables appearing in the first argument of a call to *solutions* are local. If a special goal is used, in the form *Local_vars* $\wedge$ *Goal*, then variables in the term *Local_vars* are also local, and *Goal* is used for the goal. All other variables are global. In this section, we will consider only cases where the goal is a non-variable. Any treatment of the meta-variable facilities of PROLOG should be useful for defining the semantics of *solutions* in other cases.

1.7.2.2. An Example

To illustrate how *solutions* can be used, we will use the following example.

drinks(tim, tea).   drinks(joe, tea).
drinks(tim, milk).   drinks(joe, wine).
drinks(tim, beer).

In the following queries, all variables in the goal are local.

$\leftarrow$ solutions(P, drinks(P, tea), S).
S = [tim, joe].

$\leftarrow$ solutions(P, drinks(P, wine), S).
S = [joe].

$\leftarrow$ solutions(D, P $\wedge$ drinks(P, D), S).
S = [tea, milk, beer, wine].

When there are global variables in the goal (P in the following example), there can be several solutions:

$\leftarrow$ solutions(D, drinks(P, D), S).
P = tim, S = [tea, milk, beer] ;
P = joe, S = [tea, wine]

Solutions can also be called recursively:

$\leftarrow$ solutions(D-PF.PR, solutions(P, drinks(P, D), PF.PR), S).
S = [tea-[tim, joe], milk-[tim], beer-[tim], wine-[joe]].

1.7.2.3. Implementations

Many all-solutions predicates have been implemented. In this section we describe a selection of them, concentrating of the differences with the *solutions* predicate we have described so far.

Findall

This is one of the simplest implementations, defined in PROLOG in [Clocksin 84]. The main difference between *findall* and *solutions* is the way local variables are distinguished. All variables which are unbound at the time of the call are treated as local. This ensures that calls to *findall* are deterministic.

Collect

The behaviour of *collect* [Kahn 84] is the same as *findall* except that it has features which permit more flexible control of the execution. The solutions can be computed in a lazy, as needed, fashion or eagerly, using a separate process.

All

This implementation is given in [Pereira 81] and also uses the same default as *findall* for local variables, but it can be overridden. Using a goal of the form *Goal same Global_vars*, forces variables in the term *Global_vars* to be global. Empty lists of solutions are never returned; *all* just fails in this case. One version of this predicate also removes duplicates from the list of solutions. If two solutions can be unified, only the result (sometimes less general) is put in the list of solutions.

Bagof

This is provided in DEC-10 PROLOG [Bowen 82] and has the convention for declaring local variables we have adopted for *solutions*. Like *all*, *bagof* fails if there are no solutions to the goal.

Setof

Setof [Warren 82] is the same as *bagof* except that the list of solutions is sorted and duplicates are removed. Unlike *all*, the most general solutions are retained.

Quantified-bag-of

This is available as part of the LM-PROLOG's "DEC-10 compatibility package" [Carlsson 83], and is intended to be equivalent to *bagof*. However, according to our reading of the manual, the treatment of local variables is similar to *all*, rather than *bagof*.

Quantified-set-of

This is the same as *quantified-bag-of*, except that duplicates are removed.

Set Expressions

In IC-PROLOG's set expressions [Clark 80], variables that only occur within the set expression are considered local, and the others are global. If a proof of the goal is found in which a global variable is bound, the execution terminates with a control error. Set expression (and some variants) have also been incorporated in some parallel logic programming languages, such as Parlog [Clark 83a]. These languages are beyond the scope of this thesis.

Set_of_all

Rather than return a list, this proposed predicate† returns a set of solutions. Sets must be implemented as a primitive data type of PROLOG.

1.7.3. Problems with Previous Work

1.7.3.1. Declarative Semantics

If the convention of *findall* is used to determine what variables are local, then it is generally not possible to determine what relation is computed from the program text. The semantics of the call depends on which variables are local, and this depends on the variable bindings when the call is executed. For example, the *var* predicate can be defined as follows:

var(X) :- findall(_, (X=1 ; X=2), [_, _]).

If X is a variable when var(X) is called, it will be treated as a local variable. Two solutions to the goal $\exists X$ (X=1 $\vee$ X=2) are found and var(X) succeeds. If X is not a variable, however, it acts as a global variable and the goal has one solution at most, so the call fails. Declarative semantics can be given only if it is known exactly which variables will be bound at the time of the call. Variables that appear only in the call to *solutions* cannot be bound, but the bindings of other variables depend on the order of calls. Calls to *all* can be made safe by explicitly declaring all these variables to be global.

With *setof*, etc., local variables can be determined from the program text so the semantics are clear. However, if local variables appear outside the call they may become bound and change the *setof* call. Ensuring that variables declared to be local are indeed local should be done when a program is read. Unfortunately, current implementations do not do this.

1.7.3.2. Negation

Negation (as failure) can be expressed with *solutions* by stating that the list of solutions is empty:

---

† Shimon Cohen's USENET communication, message 15987@sri-arpa, 24-Jan-1984.

not(X) :- solutions(_, X, []).

With most implementations, this behaves in the same way as the normal (unsound) PROLOG *not*. If some instance of X can be proved then *not* fails (it should fail only if all instances of X can be proved). *Set expressions* are an exception: they abort rather than failing incorrectly. The error amounts to implementing the wrong quantifier or treating global variables as local. The precise origins of the error will be discussed later, but it is due to the way negation is implemented inside *solutions*, not the high level question of how local variables are distinguished.

Another instance of the fault is illustrated by one of our previous examples: ← solutions(D, drinks(P,D), S). We neglected to mention the infinite set of answers of the form S=[], P= anything except tim and joe. Empty lists of solutions exemplify a more general problem, and failing in this particular case does not prevent non-logical behaviour. For example, *not* and *var* can be implemented with *bagof* by adding a dummy solution to the goal, as follows.

not(X) :- bagof(_, (1=1 ; X), [_]).

var(X) :- not(not(X=1)), not(not(X=2)).

1.7.3.3. Lists are Not Sets

Set expressions avoid the non-logical behaviour mentioned so far, but *var* can still be implemented, using the fact that *set expressions* return lists instead of sets. Consider the following program (we will use DEC-10 syntax but assume IC-PROLOG behaviour).

```
one_two(_, 1).        two_one(_, 2).
one_two(_, 2).        two_one(_, 1).
```

var(X) :- set_expr(Y, (two_one(X,Y), one_two(X,Y)), [1,2]).

The two solutions of the goal, Y=1 and Y=2, are fixed by the logic of the program, but the order in which they are found is not. By using IC-PROLOG's control facilities, it is possible to force *one_two* to be called first if, X is a variable, and *two_one* to be called first, if X is a non-variable (leading to the same solutions in the reverse order). The same can obviously be done with implementations like *bagof*, if sufficient control facilities are provided.

This illustrates a difficulty with Clark's specification. For an implementation to be complete, all permutations of the list of solutions must be returned.

1.7.3.4. Variables in Answers

Global variables make sorting and removing duplicates from the list of solutions difficult. Suppose there are two answers to the goal, f(X) and f(1), where X is a global variable. *Setof* has to make deterministic choices: whether to remove one answer, and the order of the answers. However, the subsequent computation may be nondeterministic, with X being bound to terms less than, equal to and greater than 1. The answer returned by *setof* must be wrong in some cases. The non-logical behaviour of *all* tends to be worse than *setof*, since the way in which duplicates are removed can cause global variables to become bound.

Local variables (actually copies of them) may also occur in answers. Because they can never become bound, it is possible to sort the list deterministically and remove duplicates correctly. The concept of duplicates must be extended to cover terms being *as general* as other terms. This is also important in finding a total order over terms containing variables. *All* and *setof* do not even distinguish between local and global variables in solutions. Again, *all* seems worse, since some solutions to the goal may be lost from the list because the least general solutions are retained.

A more fundamental objection to local variables in lists of solutions appears if the semantics are examined more closely. Consider the following goal.

← solutions(Y, X∧(Y=f(X)), S), member(f(1), S), member(f(2), S).

The call to *solutions* binds S to [f(X1)]. This has been considered an (imperfect) way to represent the infinite list of answers. The first call to *member* succeeds correctly (whatever its argument to f is) but the second call fails, despite f(1) and f(2) both being solutions to the goal. From a declarative point of view, the system proves ∀X1 solutions(Y, X∧(Y=f(X)), [f(X1)]). That is, for all X1, f(X1) is the only solution to the goal. This is obviously wrong.

1.7.4. A Sound Implementation

We first discuss the representation of sets and adapt Clark's specification, then show how the problems with variables and negation can be solved.

1.7.4.1. Representation of Sets

For goals that fail, or have only one solution, the specification can be implemented efficiently. This is sufficient for an implementation of *not*. In general though, it is clearly unacceptable to return N! answers to *solutions* when the goal has N solutions. A possibility, which prevents abuse of *bagof* etc., is to return some "random" permutation of the list of solution found. Such an implementation would be incomplete but still useful, while discouraging dependence on the order of elements in the list. An incomplete *solutions* predicate is probably less harmful than other non-logical primitives.

By using sets, *set_of_all* need not return several permutations, but it causes similar inefficiency at a later stage. For some operations on sets, such as finding the cardinality, deterministic built-in predicates could be provided, but a more general access predicate is also needed. To access all members of a set, one at a time, the obvious choice is a predicate such as *one_of(E, S, Sr)*, where *Sr* is the set *S* with element *E* deleted. To behave logically, this predicate must be nondeterministic when called with only S bound. During typical processing of a set of N elements, *one_of* is called N times, still resulting in N! solutions.

The solution we propose is to change the specification, so only one list, the canonical list, is a solution. This list is sorted with respect to some arbitrary total order over terms, and duplicate elements are removed. Removing duplicates can save processing time and the best way to do this is to sort the solutions (hence the design of *setof*). The new specification is as follows.

solutions(T, G, S) ⟷
    ∀X(∃ L_1,..,L_n(G ∧ X=T) ⟷ member(X, S)) ∧ sorted(S)

Sorted(S) is true if S is a sorted list without duplicates. One consequence of sorting the lists is that the first element is unknown until all solutions are found, so lazy evaluation is not feasible.

1.7.4.2. Removing Duplicates and Sorting

We propose two methods for sorting lists containing global variables, both of which use coroutines. The first is to delay (part of) the sorting until the global variables are sufficiently instantiated to make it deterministic. The second is to return several solutions to *sorted* and delay some tests that check the order is correct when global variables become bound. This method is more flexible and easier to implement, though the extra nondeterminism could make it less efficient. It turned out to be a very natural solution in our prototype implementation in MU-PROLOG, which we discuss further in the second part of this thesis.

Infinite sets of solutions, caused by local variables, cannot be represented by simple lists. Perhaps some form of object oriented programming would be helpful here. For our specification, however, local variables in answers must be considered an error. Ideally, the error should be flagged at the latest possible stage. Examples in our next section show how answers containing local variables lead to failure when the list is compared with nil. The result is sensible behaviour without incorrect answers.

In practical systems, some compromise between clear semantics and power or expressiveness is inevitable. The presence of local variables cannot be abused to implement *var* etc. and, we believe, very rarely causes any trouble. Moreover, it is useful for meta-level applications, such as collecting lists of program clauses. Local variables appear in answers when the goal is true for all instances of those variables. With the current specification, this implies that for all instances of those variables, there should be a corresponding element in the answer list. It would be possible to change the specification, in a rather complicated way, so that a goal being true for all occurrences of local variables implies the existence of a single corresponding element in the answer list. It is important that the sorting be extended also, or *var* can be implemented.

1.7.4.3. Negation

Problems with negation occur when global variables appear in a call to *solutions*, making it (potentially) nondeterministic. The way *solutions* is normally implemented is that for each solution to the goal, the values of the global variables and the term being collected are stored. These pairs are put into a list, from which the answers to *solutions* are extracted, by picking all elements with the same values for global variables. To make the following *pick* procedure simpler, we will make no assumptions about when the lists are sorted. We use the '-' functor to construct the pairs. It binds more strongly than '.'.

```
pick([ ], _, [ ]).
pick(Term-Glob.Sets, Glob, Term.Set) :-
        pick(Sets, Glob, Set).
pick(Term-Glob1.Sets, Glob, Set) :-
        noteq(Glob1, Glob),
        pick(Sets, Glob, Set).
```

The logic is very simple. Each term in the list of all solutions is in the answer list, if and only if the corresponding global variable values are the current global variable values. The fact that the current values are unknown at the time of the call should not bother declarative programmers! We illustrate how *pick* is used by one of our previous examples.

← pick([tea-tim, tea-joe, milk-tim, wine-joe, beer-tim], P, S).
    P = tim, S = [tea, milk, beer];
    P = joe, S = [tea, wine]

If *noteq* is defined in the same way as PROLOG's ordinary inequality (\=), no more solutions are found (in fact, the second solution is found only if *noteq* is called after *pick*, which is less efficient). The goals ← noteq(tim, P) and ← noteq(joe, P) both fail incorrectly. Using the sound implementation of inequality discussed earlier, these calls would be delayed until P is further instantiated. This leads to the answer S=[], with the two calls to *noteq* delayed. This is a reasonable representation of the infinite set of answers and behaves correctly when part of a larger computation in which P becomes bound. When empty lists of solutions are not wanted, this should be stated explicitly, as we have done with our recursive *solutions* example in Section 1.7.2.2. The following example illustrates another feature which *noteq* needs to provide.

← solutions(_, $X \wedge (Y=f(X))$, []), Y=f(Z).

The semantics of the *solutions* call are $\neg \exists X\ Y=f(X)$, so the goal should fail. The implementation results in the following call to *pick*, with two solutions.

← pick([_-f(X1)], Y, S).
    S = [_], Y = f(X1);
    S = [], noteq(f(X1), Y) (delayed).

The first solution leads to failure, since the set must be empty, avoiding a potentially incorrect answer containing local variables. The second solution leads to the goal ← noteq(f(X1), f(Z)), which we also wish to fail. Here again, we need to distinguish between local and global variables. The semantics we want are $\neg \exists X1\ f(X1)=f(Z)$ or, equivalently, $\forall X1\ f(X1) \neq f(Z)$, since the solution to the goal, Y=f(X) is true for all X. In general, variables in the first argument of *noteq* should be considered universally quantified. This is true even if they are copies of global variables, as our final example in this section shows.

← solutions(_, X=f(Y), []).

This leads to the following call to *pick*.

← pick([_-f(Y1).Y1], X.Y, S).
    S = [_], X = f(Y1), Y = Y1;
    S = [], noteq(f(Y1).Y1, X.Y) (delayed).

We use '.' to group the two global variables, though any functor would do. The semantics of the delayed call are $\forall Y1\ f(Y1).Y1 \neq X.Y$, which is equivalent to $f(Y) \neq X$, as desired. *Noteq* can be implemented efficiently in the way discussed earlier. Our current implementation is not based on ~=, due to the difficulty of manipulating underscores that we mentioned. Instead, we have written a prototype in MU-PROLOG, using wait declarations to cause delays. It is generally much slower than ~=, which is implemented in C, but it does maintain term frontiers, so the order of efficiency is sometimes better.

1.7.5. Application to Negation

Our proposed implementation of *solutions*, with the definition of *not* given in Section 1.7.3.2, make an interesting implementation of negation. The call to *not* is effectively replaced by an equivalent conjunction of calls to *noteq*. One call is generated for each solution to the goal. The computation below illustrates this.

← not member(X, [1,2,3]).

. . .

← pick([_-1,_-2,_-3], X, [ ]).

. . .

← noteq(1, X), noteq(2, X), noteq(3, X).

Consider the following three examples:

← not member(1, [f(Z),2]).   (1)

This gets converted into an empty conjunction. That is, the computation succeeds. With delaying until ground, the call causes incompleteness if Z is never bound. Also, within a nondeterministic computation, the call may be done several times.

← not member(1, [1,X]).   (2)

This get converted into ← noteq(X1, X), which immediately fails. If *not* is delayed until the call is ground, the failure is not detected as quickly.

← not member(1, [X,Y]).   (3)

It is impossible to tell if this call should succeed or fail until it is further instantiated. This means that IC-PROLOG's *not*, which works well with the previous two examples, will abort. With the all solutions *not*, the call is converted into the following goal, and both calls delay.

← noteq(1.Y1, X.Y), noteq(X1.1, X.Y).

If either X or Y get bound to 1, the calls will be resumed and one will fail (as in case 2). If X is bound to f(Z) and Y is bound to 2, the calls will be resumed and both will succeed (as in case 1). This form of negation, therefore, has the advantages of IC-PROLOG's *not*, but is more flexible in the way it is called. As long as the goal has a finite number of solutions, no difficulties arise. From a control point of view, this makes it much easier to use (see Part II of this thesis).

[Kahn 84] shows how an all solutions predicate can be used to implement *cases* and other constructs related to negation. Of course, these can behave non-logically unless the all solutions predicate is implemented correctly. With *solutions*, implicit negations are converted into calls to *noteq*, in the same way as above.

1.7.6. Summary

Previous work on all solutions predicates has resulted in a large number of implementations, which can all behave non-logically, and a specification which cannot be implemented efficiently. The specification can be improved by forcing the solution list to be sorted and duplicates removed. Allowing local variables in the answer does make the predicate more useful, though the specification, and possibly the object returned, needs to be considerably more complex.

Our proposed implementation uses the same convention as *bagof* for distinguishing local variables. In addition, when the program is read, it should be ensured that variables declared to be local are indeed so. The implementation relies on the ability to use coroutines, for sorting lists of solutions containing global variables and for the implementation of a sound form of inequality. The inequality predicate must allow some variables to be universally quantified. *Solutions* has well defined declarative semantics and its efficiency can be comparable with current implementations.

1.8. Negative Unifiers

The idea of negative unifiers is similar to our all solutions *not*, but negative information is incorporated into unifiers, instead of separate calls to an inequality predicate. For example, in the call below, the three solutions to *member* would be found, then the negation of each one would be added to the unifier. The final substitution (using the notation of [Khabaza 84]) is {~{X/1}, ~{X/2}, ~{X/3}}.

　　　← not member(X, [1,2,3]).

The unifier can become a very complex expression, with nested negated and positive components. Whenever a variable is bound, or a call to *not* is completed, we need to recompute part or all of the unifier. [Khabaza 84] suggests keeping the unifier in disjunctive normal form, to simplify this. One advantage of the method, is that nested negations can be handled. With the all solutions method, delayed inequalities in an inner negation cause the outer negation to abort.

It is not clear how large the implementation overhead for negative unifiers would be. For a compiler based system, it would probably be significant and the benefit would not be outstanding. A system that supports coroutining may have a similar overhead, but it allows several different forms of negation and better control facilities to be implemented. Also, it is not clear if, or how, universal quantifiers could be incorporated into a scheme with negative unifiers. It may be necessary to make unifiers even more complex.

1.9. Program Transformation

Program transformation techniques can be used to implement negation using inequality. The effect is like our all solutions negation, but the control is simplified. Predicate definitions are transformed so they compute the negation of the original predicate. The negated version relies on ~= to fail when the original would succeed and vice versa. It is important that we take the semantics of a program to be its completion, since a predicate must be completely defined before we can compute its complement. Throughout the transformation process, it is also necessary to keep track of the different quantifiers in the formulas being manipulated. We will now outline how the standard definition of *member* can be negated.

Predicate Definition

```
member(A, A.B).
member(A, B.C) :- member(A, C).
```

Completed Definition

∀ A,B member(A, B) ⟷ ∃ C,D (B=C.D ∧ A=C
    ∨ B=C.D ∧ E=A ∧ member(E, D))

Negated Completion

∀ A,B notmember(A, B) ⟷ ¬∃ C,D (B=C.D ∧ A=C
    ∨ B=C.D ∧ E=A ∧ member(E, D))

⟷ ¬∃ C,D (B=C.D ∧ (A=C ∨ member(A, D)))
⟷ ¬∃ C,D (B=C.D) ∨ ∃ C,D (B=C.D ∧ ¬(A=C ∨ member(A, D)))
⟷ ∀ X,Y (B≠X.Y) ∨ ∃ C,D (B=C.D ∧ A≠C ∧ notmember(A, D)))

Negated Definition

notmember(A, B) :- B ~= _._.
notmember(A, B.C) :- A ~= B, notmember(A, C).

Any negated call to *member* in the program is changed to a call to *notmember*. This is a very simple (but useful) example of a transformation. One thing that makes some derivations much more complex, is the presence of variables which appear in the body of clauses, but not in the head [Sato 84]. The solution offered by [Sato 84], is to use a general purpose program transformation system, such as that described in [Tamaki 84], which uses fold and unfold transformations. [Schultz 84] gives negating transformations as an application of another system for more general transformation of first order logic programs. The space of equivalent programs is searched for one which can be written with horn clauses plus inequality. Shultz shows such a program can always be found, but the system has not yet been developed as a practical tool. Some heuristics to guide the search in larger examples would be useful.

The transformation process can sometimes be simplified if a system of typed logic is used. This is assumed by [Sato 84], and one of the consequences is that some inequalities with universal quantifiers can be eliminated. For example, if the second argument of *member* must be a list, *notmember* can be written as follows.

notmember(A, []).
notmember(A, B.C) :- A ~= B, notmember(A, C).

Types may also be used to distinguish database and other procedures, which are more suited to the delaying until ground negation. Transforming database procedures results in large conjunctions of inequalities, and the benefits of database indexing are lost. Later, we give another application of types to negation. Regardless of whether types are used, this form of negation should be pursued because it has significant advantages over other implementations for recursive programs.

When a negated goal has a finite number of solutions, the transformation method works in a similar way to *solutions* but with fewer overheads. Several calls to ~= are made, which are equivalent to the negated call. The three *not member* goals we gave when discussing *solutions* result in equivalent, though slightly simpler inequalities. For the goal below, however, the behaviour is far superior.

← not member(1, 1.X).

Because the negated goal has an infinite number of solutions, *solutions* and negative unifiers would result in an infinite loop. With program transformation, the call quickly fails. One can prove that for any call to *member*, if its universal closure is true, the corresponding *notmember* call fails, and if *member* fails then the *notmember* call has one solution. The following negated goal has an infinite number of solutions, all of which bind X.

← not member(1, 2.X).

The resulting call to *notmember* also has an infinite number of solutions. However, since it is a normal PROLOG call, rather than being within some form of *not*, this control problem can be handled with the rest of the computation. There is no inner and outer computation dichotomy. In Part II, we show how control information can be added to *notmember* automatically, so it delays when its second argument is a variable. In this way, an efficient "incremental" version of *not member* can be implemented. Whenever the list is further instantiated, *notmember* wakes up and calls ~=, to check that the new element is not equal to the first argument. The same kind of incremental behaviour is also exhibited by other predicates similarly transformed.

1.9.1. Functions

We now describe a new transformation technique that can be used to implement negation with ~= in some special cases. The negated predicate must act as a total function for some input–output mode. That is, some subset of its arguments are a function of the rest of the arguments. However, its use is not restricted to this mode. Consider the standard *append* predicate:

append([ ], A, A).
append(A.B, C, A.D) :– append(B, C, D).

The third argument of *append* is a function of the first two arguments. Because the function should be total, *append* must not be called with a non-list as its first argument. If the transformation is used just as a programming technique, this sort of restriction rarely matters. However, to automate the process, some sort of type system is needed. Also, some help from the programmer may be needed to detect functions. Perhaps the technique would be best suited to some combination of logic and functional programming. The transformation for *append* is as follows:

not append(A, B, C) ====> append(A, B, D), D ~= C.

This transformation can be used for all negated calls to *append*, or for defining a *notappend* predicate, like the approach in the previous section:

notappend(A, B, C) :– append(A, B, D), D ~= C.

Sometimes there are several functions associated with one predicate, so more than one transformation is possible. In the following program, which appends a single element to a list, the third argument is a function of the first two, and the first two arguments are a function of the third. Both these functions can be used to implement negation.

append1([ ], A, [A]).
append1(A.B, C, A.D) :– append1(B, C, D).

not append1(A, B, C) ====> append1(A, B, D), D ~= C.
not append1(A, B, C) ====> append1(D, E, C), D.E ~= A.B.

In general, the negation is removed, the vector of output arguments are replaced by a vector of distinct variables and a call to ~= is added, to ensure the two vectors are different. Assuming functions can be found, this is very easy to apply and has many of the advantages of the other transformation method we discussed, such as detecting failure as soon as possible. The following proposition shows that the transformation preserves equivalence.

<u>Proposition</u> If a predicate p obeys the following axioms (where x, y and z denote vectors of variables)

1) $\forall x \exists y \ p(x,y)$

2) $\forall x \forall y \forall z(p(x,y) \wedge p(x,z) \rightarrow y=z)$

3) The standard equality axioms

then

$\forall x \forall y(\neg p(x,y) \longleftrightarrow \exists z(p(x,z) \wedge y \neq z)$ holds.

<u>Proof</u> Suppose $\neg p(s,t)$ is true. By axiom one, there exist u such that $p(s,u)$ is true. This implies that if u=t, then $p(s,t)$ is true (by the equality axioms). Therefore, u does not equal t, since $p(s,t)$ and $\neg p(s,t)$ cannot both be true. Suppose $p(s,u) \wedge u \neq t$ is true. By the contrapositive of axiom two, $\neg p(s,t) \vee \neg p(s,u)$ is true. Therefore, $\neg p(s,t)$ is true, since $\neg p(s,u)$ is false. □

The following example shows how failure is detected as soon as possible (the negated call does not need to be ground). The single solution to the *append1* call binds D to [A,B], and ~= immediately fails.

not append1([A], B, [A,B]) ====> append1([A], B, D), D ~= [A,B].

Where there are an infinite number of solutions, which all bind variables in the goal, then some calls must delay. The simplest case is when only the call to ~= needs to delay. In the next example, *append1* binds D to [C,B] and [C,B] ~= [A,B] delays. If C is subsequently bound to A, then ~= will fail.

not append1([C], B, [A,B]) ====> append1([C], B, D), D ~= [A,B].

If the first argument of *append1* is a variable, then the transformed goal can have an infinite number of solutions:

not append1(C, B, [A,B]) ====> append1(C, B, D), D ~= [A,B].

With the control we suggest in Part II, *append1*, as well as ~=, would delay. If C is then bound to [A], the call would be resumed and execution would proceed as before.

The next example shows how success can also be found quickly. The *append1* call has one solution and binds D to [1,A], then ~= succeeds.

not append1([1], A, 2.3.B) ====> append1([1], A, D), D ~= 2.3.B.

However, successful goals do not always behave so nicely. Consider the example below.

not append1(1.A, B, 2.C) ====> append1(1.A, B, D), D ~= 2.C.

The transformed *append1* goal has an infinite number of solutions. The only way to avoid them, is to wait for A to become more instantiated. In part II, we show how to implement this, but it does not help if A never becomes sufficiently instantiated. However, the behaviour is still much better than delaying until ground.

A possible solution to this is to consider only the first answer to the goal. Since D does not appear elsewhere, completeness is not compromised. However, the common implementation of this can behave non-logically. The simplest way we know of implementing it soundly is to use double negation with quantifiers, but that is of no use when we are trying to implement negation. Another extension that could improve efficiency in this example is lazy evaluation of the call to *append1*. Its only use in the computation is to produce D for the call to ~=. As soon as D is bound to 2.D1, the inequality succeeds. There is no point in further instantiating D to 2.3.D2, etc. Since the function is total, we know the call has a solution, so it can be aborted.

Both of these extensions can be implemented by further transformations. We have not fully investigated this area, so we cannot say how often it can be done without too much difficulty. However, we will give on example, using the *append1* transformation above.

notappend1(A, B, C) :- append1(A, B, D), D ~= C.

First, we apply an unfold transformation, using the definition of *append1*.

notappend1([ ], A, B) :- B ~= [A].
notappend1(A.B, C, D) :- append1(B, C, E), D ~= A.E.

The call to ~= in the second clause can now be expanded, like an unfold transformation:

notappend1([ ], A, B) :- B ~= [A].
notappend1(A.B, C, D) :- append1(B, C, E), D ~= _._.
notappend1(A.B, C, D.F) :- append1(B, C, E), D ~= A.
notappend1(A.B, C, A.D) :- append1(B, C, E), D ~= E.

With this program, we can simply implement the two enhancements. Firstly, the idea of lazy evaluation can be implemented by noting that the calls to *append1* in the second and third clauses must succeed (since E only appears in those subgoals). The subgoals can therefore be deleted. Secondly, the infinite number of solutions to the *append1* call may then be avoided by applying a fold transformation to the last clause:

notappend1([ ], A, B) :- B ~= [A].
notappend1(A.B, C, D) :- D ~= _._.
notappend1(A.B, C, D.F) :- D ~= A.
notappend1(A.B, C, A.D) :- notappend1(B, C, D).

This is an efficient incremental version of *notappend1*, which has no trouble with infinite numbers of solutions (assuming sensible control). The transformation techniques used here are being explored further.

1.10. Conclusions

Nearly all sound implementations of negation as failure rely on the ability to delay calls, until certain variables are bound. With such a mechanism available, implementing a version of *not* that delays until it is ground is fairly simple. Implementing inequality is also easy. Because it is such a common use of negation, and it is important in many of the more sophisticated implementations of *not*, the more advanced implementation is warranted. With very little extra work, both of these forms of negation can be extended, to support universally quantified variables. This considerably increases expressive power and usefulness. Reliance on the unsound implementations is also avoided. Perhaps surprisingly, this has been supported by very few implementations in the past. *If-then-else* can be implemented in a similar way to *not*, thus providing an alternative to the use of cuts in many situations.

Delaying until ground is generally the most efficient form of negation for database style programming, and the restrictions are rarely any trouble. However, delaying until ground often prevents early detection of failure when programming with recursive data structures, thus introducing inefficiency. A simple incremental version of *not* seems impossible, but there is a spectrum of other options, ranging from IC-PROLOG's *not* to *solutions* and negative unifiers. Negative unifiers can handle nested negations, but universal quantifiers are not supported. A sound all solutions predicate is very useful in its own right and can also be used for negation. All these methods require good control to avoid infinite loops, inefficiency or abnormal termination. This can be largely overcome by our ideas for retrying *not* and dealing with infinite numbers of solutions, though some computation is duplicated.

By far the most promising treatment of negation for recursive predicates, is program transformation. More work is needed to produce practical systems, but many simple programs can be transformed adequately already. The control needed is much simpler because there is no inner and outer computation. The transformed predicates can therefore proceed incrementally.

We suggest the following implementations of negation be incorporated into PROLOG systems of the future:

(1) Versions of *not* and *if-then-else* that support universal quantifiers and which delay until ground.

(2) An inequality predicate with universal quantifiers. The more efficient implementation we described should be used.

(3) A soundly implemented all solutions predicated with well defined semantics.

Some analysis of the types in the program could be used to distinguish between database and recursive predicates. The former should use the delay until ground negation and the latter should be transformed, if possible. If suitable transformations cannot be found, delaying until ground or *solutions* could be used. If finding transformations is often too difficult, the version of *not* that is retried should be implemented. One of the last two methods we suggested for dealing with infinite numbers of solutions should also be incorporated.

PART II – CONTROL OF LOGIC PROGRAMS

2. INTRODUCTION

A major goal of logic programming research, is to build systems that will efficiently solve problems stated in simple logic. This cannot easily be realised in conventional PROLOG systems (for example, DEC-10 PROLOG [Bowen 82]), due to the the lack of control facilities. Poor control facilities lead to infinite loops and inefficiency. To overcome this, it is often necessary to make the logic more complex. There is now a growing number of PROLOG-based systems (and proposed systems) with extra control facilities, to enable coroutining. Examples are IC-PROLOG [Clark 79], Epilog [Porto 82], Two Level PROLOG [Porto 84], PROLOG-II [Colmerauer 82], LM-PROLOG [Carlsson 83] and MU-PROLOG [Naish 85a]. The advantage of such systems is that it is possible to make programs efficient by adding control information, rather than changing the logic [Kowalski 79].

The next chapter contains our main contribution to the area. We show how the addition of control information can often be automated. This is a significant new step in the direction of making the task of programming simpler. We give a model of the execution of our MU-PROLOG system, and introduce two control primitives. Heuristics are given for applying them to database and recursive procedures. This leads to algorithms for generating control information, and a preprocessor for logic programs which we have developed.

In the following chapter, we re-examine the theoretical foundations of systems such as MU-PROLOG. Previous work made a over-simplification in the definition of computation rules. We overcome this problem by defining Heterogeneous SLD resolution, which is a generalisation of SLD resolution. Soundness and completeness results are shown to still hold. The more rigorous treatment of the refutation procedure also leads us to new possibilities in computation rules. We give one rule which can behave like a simple form of intelligent backtracking and can dynamically reorder subgoals, to initiate coroutining between generators and tests.

In our final chapter, we present a broad overview of the many proposals for control. Two features of computations rules are used to evaluate and classify them. The first is the well known idea of detecting failure as soon as possible (where it is unavoidable). The second idea is to avoid failures. The extend to which various language constructs and heuristics embody these two ideas is discussed. By examining current systems in this light, several conclusions are reached. These concern deficiencies in the performance of the systems and how they may be overcome. We propose an idealized system with a hierarchy of goals and a fair computation rule. Some modifications needed in a practical implementation are also considered.

3. AUTOMATING CONTROL

3.1. Introduction

There are now many control primitives, implemented or proposed, but little work has been done on developing methodologies for their use. It has always been assumed that the control information is to be added by programmers, and the only guidance given to them has been a small set of examples. In this chapter, we introduce two control primitives and a methodology for using them. The methodology can be used to generate control information automatically in many cases. We show how this work can be incorporated into a program that takes as input a logic program, and outputs an equivalent MU-PROLOG program, with control information added. The control primitives are fairly simple, compared to some, but we believe this approach will be very rewarding. In fact, the automation of control can be applied to forms of compilation and program transformation [Gregory 80] [Bellia 83] as well as execution, as we discuss here.

We first present a general model of the execution mechanism of MU-PROLOG. To show how the control is used, three classes of predicates are then discussed. These are system predicates, database predicates, and a class of recursively-defined predicates. Control heuristics are given for database and recursive procedures, which lead to algorithms that generate control information, using the two new primitives. Methods for reordering subgoals are also given. Next, we describe how the algorithms can be used in a preprocessor for logic programs. We give examples of how the preprocessor is useful for a variety of programming styles. We also discuss the possibility of other control primitives being generated automatically.

3.2. The Execution Model

PROLOG's computation rule can be changed to improve efficiency and avoid non-termination without affecting correctness (see [Lloyd 84b]). In conventional PROLOG systems, a depth first, left to right computation rule is used to select subgoals, and each call either succeeds or fails. In our model, calls may also delay, and be resumed at a later point. The delaying of calls causes no bindings so, in effect, it just changes the computation rule. The default rule still selects the left-most goal at each stage.

In MU-PROLOG, all information controlling delaying is attached to procedures, rather than calls. Some advantages of this are:

(1)   greater modularity (a procedure and its control information form a module),

(2)   greater separation of control information from the logic, and

(3)   less duplication when the same control is desired for several calls, which is quite common.

A disadvantage is that different calls to the same procedure cannot have different control. However, it is much easier to implement control on calls using control on procedures than vice versa.

Control is also local, in the sense that it can apply only to a single procedure. There are no control primitives which can affect calls to more than one procedure. This limits the power of the control but the implementation is significantly less expensives, and automatic generation of non-local control is likely to be more difficult.

There are several possible reasons for delaying a call, all involving the presence of one or more variables in the call. Some calls to system predicates delay because the presence of variables makes the result of a call difficult or impossible to compute. In other cases, delaying a call until some variables are bound can increase efficiency or prevent an infinite loop. Whatever the reason, the offending variables are marked, to indicate that the call is waiting for them to be bound. If a marked variable is bound at any stage, all the calls waiting for it are woken up. Some calls may also wake if all the non-delayed calls have completed (see Section 3.3.4).

At any point in a PROLOG computation, there is a current goal clause. In MU-PROLOG there is also a set of delayed calls. As an example, we will use the goal clause containing the atoms P, Q and R, with atoms S and T delayed. This will be represented by the following notation:

$\leftarrow$ P, Q, R   &   S, T.

P is now chosen, since it is the left-most goal. If it delays, it is simply transferred from the left of the goal clause to the set of delayed calls:

$\leftarrow$ Q, R   &   S, T, P.

This is logically identical to the previous clause but now Q will be called. In effect, the computation rule selects Q instead of P. Suppose it matches a clause containing the atoms U and V. The computation rule is depth-first, so these replace Q at the left of the goal:

$\leftarrow$ U, V, R   &   S, T, P.

Now suppose U matches a clause containing the atom W, and in doing so it binds some marked variables which S and P are waiting on. These two calls are woken and are placed at the left of the goal, in the order in which they were delayed, and U is replaced by W:

$\leftarrow$ S, P, W, V, R   &   T.

The computation is now continued normally, the next call being S. Woken calls are likely to be tests, so it is important that they be put at the start of the goal and hence resumed as soon as possible. In IC-PROLOG, the calls are woken in the reverse order. [Clark 83b] gives an example to support this, but there are equally valid examples which support our method. Actually, the order in which calls are resumed rarely makes much difference since tests require relatively little computation.

When a goal fails, we backtrack to the most recent call which has alternative clauses to try. Points where calls were delayed are ignored, since logically, delays have no effect. The computation may terminate in one of three ways; we may backtrack past the initial goal (failure), we may reach the empty goal clause (success), or we may reach a goal containing only delayed calls, none of which get woken. This last case can be treated as a control error and, with well-written programs, it usually indicates that the goal has an infinite number of solutions.

3.3. System Predicates

The delaying mechanism outlined above is useful for many of the system predicates. A very useful application is for the implementation of negation, as we have seen. This is used in MU-PROLOG, for ~ (not), *if-then-else*, and ~= (not equals). Using these predicates, instead of their unsoundly implemented counterparts, ensures the correctness of answers. Many meta-logical predicates, such as *name* and *functor*, also delay rather than cause errors, or just fail. This enables greater programming flexibility while maintaining correctness. The same applies for calls to the arithmetic predicates such as <, which delays until both its arguments are ground, and *plus*, which delays until at least two arguments are ground. Delaying insufficiently instantiated calls to system predicates can also be used to increase efficiency.

3.4. Database Procedures

A database procedure is made up of a (generally large) collection of ground, unit clauses. An important application of such procedures is in deductive database systems (see [Lloyd 83], [Dahl 82]). A flexible computation rule in this context can be used for query optimization, and similar control is also useful for smaller collections of facts stored in main memory. The control regime we suggest extends the method of query optimization used in CHAT-80 [Warren 81] and generalised in [Stabler 83]. Both these systems rely on static analysis and reordering of the initial query and/or the bodies of rules in the program. In contrast, the method we present is part of the computation rule of the interpreter.

Central to all these systems is a method of estimating the number of solutions to an arbitrary call to a database procedure. This can be seen as the number of clauses in the procedure multiplied by the probability of the subgoal matching an arbitrary clause. To simplify matters, it is assumed that the probabilities of the different arguments matching are independent. The probability of a match is then the product of the probabilities of each instantiated argument matching. The probabilities can be given by a programmer, or found by taking statistics over some period of typical usage. Alternatively, they can be estimated automatically, by taking the inverse of the number of distinct constants in each argument of the procedure.

Given an accurate estimate of the number of solutions to each call, it is possible to optimize the number of calls required to find all solutions to a database query. The number of calls is a simple indication of the time taken. Later, we shall also consider the number of unifications performed, which can vary if any form of indexing is used. At the root of the SLD tree for the goal, there is a single node. Each subsequent level has N times as many nodes as the previous level, where N is the number of solutions to the subgoal called at the previous level. For a database query consisting of M subgoals, we therefore aim to minimize

$$1 + N_1 + N_1.N_2 + \ldots + N_1.N_2...N_{M-1}$$

where N_i is the number of solutions of the ith called subgoal (after all previous subgoals have been solved). The lowest level of the tree just consists of success nodes, so it does not result in any calls. The choice of the first subgoal affects the number of solutions to subsequent calls, so simply minimizing N_1 (as CHAT-80 does) is not always optimal. Some orders result in more calls initially, but the lower levels of the tree are made smaller, because certain variables are bound.

In practice, M is usually very small, so the naive algorithm of evaluating the objective function for every order is feasible. In cases where M is larger, some approximation may be necessary. It seems very unlikely that there is an optimization algorithm with complexity polynomial in M in the worse case (though we have not proved this). However, there may be algorithms which are more efficient in practice. Almost all cases where M is large result from recursive rules. If an algorithm is devised which is exponential only in the number of different procedures called, for example, this should be sufficient.

3.4.1. Priority Declarations

The implementation we propose allows each database procedure to have a *priority declaration*, which specifies the number of clauses, and the probability of a match for each argument. As in CHAT-80, the inverse of each probability is given, to avoid fractions. The following example declares that procedure *stud_unit* has 500 clauses, and the probabilities of the first and second arguments matching a call are 1/100 and 1/10, respectively.

    ?– priority(stud_unit(100, 10), 500).

The effect of priority declarations is to delay calls to database procedures until other calls have been solved or delayed. The delayed database procedure calls are then analysed and resumed in an efficient order. In practice, delaying ground calls rarely increases efficiency (and it may complicate the implementation). Consider the following program:

    busy(P, T) :– class_time(U, T), attends(P, U).

    attends(S, U) :– stud_unit(S, U).
    attends(L, U) :– lect_unit(L, U).

    ?– priority(stud_unit(100, 10), 500).
    ?– priority(lect_unit(8, 10), 10).
    ?– priority(class_time(10, 25), 30).
    . . . .

The times each person is busy can be computed as follows:

    ← busy(P, T).
    ← class_time(U, T), attends(P, U).
    ← attends(P, U) & class_time(U, T).
    ← stud_unit(P, U) & class_time(U, T).
    ←   & class_time(U, T), stud_unit(P, U).

At this point, the delayed calls are analysed, with reference to the priority declarations. *Class_time* has fewer solutions (30 compared to 500), and it is resumed first. The call to *class_time* binds U, so the subsequent calls to *stud_unit* have an average of 500/10=50 solutions. After finding all these solutions by backtracking, the second clause for *attends* is tried, leading to the goal

    ←   & class_time(U, T), lect_unit(P, U).

Now there is a call to *lect_unit*, with only 10 solutions, instead of *stud_unit*, and it is resumed first.

This behaviour cannot be achieved by static re-ordering. *Class_time* would either be called first each time or second each time, both of which are less efficient. Similarly, without dynamic re-ordering of the goal, it would not be possible to call anything between the calls to *class_time* and *stud_unit*, even though this may be the most efficient order.

3.4.2. Minimizing the Number of Unifications

Minimizing the number of calls does not necessarily minimize the time spent executing a query, since some calls take far more time than others. For large relations, most time is spent searching for matching facts; either performing unifications or reading from disk. For a given call, the number of successful unifications is fixed, but many unsuccessful unifications can be avoided by using some form of clause indexing. Clause indexing can have a major impact on efficiency, and should be considered in any optimization scheme. Adapting our formula for the number of calls, the number of unifications (or disk accesses) needed to find all solutions to a database goal is

$$U_1 + N_1 U_2 + N_1.N_2 U_3 + \ldots + N_1.N_2...N_{M-1} U_M$$

where U_i is the number of unifications (disk accesses) performed in a single call of the ith subgoal. U_i is easily calculated with most forms of indexing, by using information on which arguments of the call are instantiated, and information in priority declarations.

Consider our previous *class_time* and *lect_unit* goal. With no indexing, if *class_time* is called first, there are 31 calls and $30+30\times10=340$ unifications performed. If *lect_unit* is called first, there are 11 calls and $10+10\times30=310$ unifications performed. If there is a simple inverted index on the second argument of *lect_unit*, however, calls to that relation with the second argument instantiated take only one unification. If *class_time* is called first, only $30+30\times1=60$ unifications are performed (the other figures remain the same). Unless the overhead of calling takes more time than ten unifications, the indexing results in a different optimal call order.

Forms of indexing and the relative costs of calls, unifications and disk accesses are implementation dependent, so no one formula can be given for query optimization. Other factors, such as the varying cost of unification, may also be worth considering. The main principle, however, is that information in priority declarations can be used to estimate the number of solutions to each call. Other information, such as the form of indexing, can be used to estimate the cost of each call. Combining these, we obtain a formula for the total cost of evaluating a query. By incorporating this knowledge into the computation rule, the efficiency can be greatly improved. MU-PROLOG has a facility for storing large database procedures in files [Naish 83b] and we plan to implement priority declarations also.

One limitation of this approach is that separate database queries are optimized independently. [Gallaire 83] discusses some other approaches which are outside the scope of SLD resolution and this thesis. They attempt to compile deductive database queries so all resulting queries on the base relations can be considered together. This enables more optimizations, but handling recursive rules is difficult. In fact, complexity arguments suggest that compilation is not always possible [de Rougemont 84], so it seems there will always be a need for some default evaluation method, at least.

3.5. Recursive Procedures

Under this heading, we include most procedures that manipulate recursive data structures, such as lists and trees. They are generally made up of a small number of clauses; some containing recursive subgoals and some being non-recursive "base cases" (for example, facts containing nil). In conventional PROLOG systems, the order of the subgoals in these procedures is very important. Often all orders cause inefficient or infinite computations for some calls.

3.5.1. Wait Declarations

In this section, a control primitive that can overcome these problems is presented. It is MU-PROLOG's *wait declaration*. An algorithm to generate wait declarations, first mentioned in [Naish 82], is then given, along with some other heuristics for improving efficiency.

We first describe wait declarations with the following example:

```
?- wait append(1, 1, 0).
?- wait append(0, 1, 1).
append([ ], A, A).
append(A.B, C, A.D) :- append(B, C, D).
```

The ones in a wait declaration define the (positions) set of arguments in a call which may be constructed. Multiple wait declarations provide alternative ways of calling procedures. The effect of these declarations is to force calls to *append* to wait until the first or third arguments do not need to be constructed.

As each argument of a call is being unified with the corresponding argument in a procedure head, we check if it is constructed. An argument of a call is *constructed* if a variable in it is unified with a non-variable. The result of a successful unification is a set of variable bindings, and a set C, of positions at which arguments were constructed. If the procedure has no wait declarations, or C is a subset of the positions set of any wait declaration, then the call succeeds; otherwise it delays. When a call delays, all the variables which were bound are reset and marked.

Consider the following call.

$\leftarrow$ append(X, 3.[ ], 1.2.3.[ ]).

Only the first argument is constructed (X is bound to A.B). The first wait declaration allows this, so the call succeeds. Similarly, the call

$\leftarrow$ append(1.2.[ ], 3.[ ], X).

constructs only the third argument (X is bound to 1.D), which is permitted by the second wait declaration. However, for the call

$\leftarrow$ append(X, 3.[ ], Y).

the first and third arguments are constructed (X and Y are bound to [] and 3.[], respectively). Because no wait declaration has ones in the first and third arguments, the call delays and X and Y are reset and marked.

Append without wait declarations can efficiently join and split lists, but when it is part of a larger program, it can cause problems, as the following procedure illustrates:

append3(A, B, D, E) :- append(A, B, C), append(C, D, E).

Without wait declarations on *append* this program works for joining lists, but not for splitting them. Consider the goal below.

← append3(X, 3.[ ], 4.[ ], 1.2.3.4.[ ]).

Successive solutions to the first call to *append* are found by backtracking. The second call keeps failing, until the first call binds X to a list of the correct length. The time taken is proportional to the square of the length, and if backtracking occurs subsequently, the further solutions to the first call cause an infinite loop. If the calls to *append* were reversed, the same problems would occur for joining lists, and if the order of the clauses of *append* were reversed, then an infinite loop would occur immediately. No order works for both splitting and joining, and some goals, such as the following one, cause infinite loops for all orders.

← append3(1.W, X, Y, 2.Z).

The behaviour of *append3* is typical of many PROLOG programs. It is usually possible to re-write these programs to make them behave better but it is often difficult (see [Elcock 83]) and is an undesirable burden on the programmer. Adding control information is far easier and the result is more readable. The following computation starts with the same goal for splitting lists, but we assume that *append* has the wait declarations given above:

← append3(X, 3.[ ], 4.[ ], 1.2.3.4.[ ]).
← append(X, 3.[ ], C), append(C, 4.[ ], 1.2.3.4.[ ]).
← append(C, 4.[ ], 1.2.3.4.[ ]) & append(X, 3.[ ], C).
← append(X, 3.[ ], 1.C1), append(C1, 4.[ ], 2.3.4.[ ]).
← append(X1, 3.[ ], C1), append(C1, 4.[ ], 2.3.4.[ ]).
. . .

In this case, the first call to *append* delays. The second call binds C to 1.C1 and wakes the delayed call. This can now proceed, binding X to 1.X1, then calling itself recursively. The two calls act as coroutines, making the time taken proportional to the length of X and avoiding the infinite loop. In fact, with wait declarations, the program works for splitting, joining and testing the front of lists, for any order of goals and clauses. Furthermore, the control information can be generated automatically, so the programmer need only consider the logic.

The reason why the program works so well is that calls to *append* with variables in the first and third arguments delay. Such calls have an infinite number of possible bindings for these arguments. Without wait declarations, this causes infinite loops and inefficient "guessing" of the length of the lists. In this lies an excellent control heuristic: calls should delay rather than "guess" one of a infinite number of possible bindings for any variable.

3.5.2. Generating Wait Declarations

It is not possible to use the heuristic mentioned above directly but wait declarations can often achieve the same result. They can easily be written by a programmer or generated automatically, which is what is discussed here. Consider the *append* program. The reason for the infinite number of solutions and infinite loop, is that the second clause can keep recursing indefinitely. Each call generates a solution and another recursive call. The wait declarations stop this by preventing the first and third arguments of a call being constructed. The method of generating wait declarations then, is to look for potentially infinite loops and add sufficient waits to prevent them. We will now show

how wait declarations can be generated for the following program, then the algorithm will be summarized.

    merge([ ], L, L).
    merge(L, [ ], L).
    merge(N.X, M.Y, N.Z) :− N < M, merge(X, M.Y, Z).
    merge(N.X, M.Y, M.Z) :− N >= M, merge(N.X, Y, Z).

Both recursive calls can lead to infinite loops. To investigate the first loop, we compare the call with the head of the clause. The first and third arguments of the call are more general than the same arguments in the head. In a call to *merge*, if either of these arguments is a list of determinate length, its length in successive recursive calls must decrease, so the recursion must terminate. If both arguments end with variables, then both are eventually constructed, the length does not decrease, and the recursion does not terminate. The least restrictive way to prevent the loop, is to delay calls which construct both arguments. In other words, only allow calls that do not construct the first argument or do not construct the third argument. This can be done with the following two wait declarations (the wait declarations of *append* can be generated in this way):

    ?− wait merge(0, 1, 1).
    ?− wait merge(1, 1, 0).

In the second loop, the second and third arguments in the call are more general than the arguments in the head. To prevent this loop, it is sufficient to have the following wait declarations.

    ?− wait merge(1, 0, 1).
    ?− wait merge(1, 1, 0).

It is now necessary to combine the two groups of wait declarations, so both loops are prevented. No wait declaration in the first group will allow the first loop. The same applies for the second group. Therefore, the set intersection of two wait declarations from the first and second groups cannot allow either loop. Including all intersections, of one wait from each group, gives the least restrictive set of wait declarations which will stop both loops:

    ?− wait merge(0, 0, 1).
    ?− wait merge(0, 1, 0).
    ?− wait merge(1, 0, 0).
    ?− wait merge(1, 1, 0).

These wait declarations delay *merge* precisely when it tries to guess one of an infinite number of possibilities. However, the second and third declarations are subsets of the fourth declaration. Any call allowed by these declarations must be allowed by the fourth declarations, so they are redundant. The final wait declarations are therefore:

    ?− wait merge(0, 0, 1).
    ?− wait merge(1, 1, 0).

With these declarations, *merge* can be used for merging the first two lists, if they are instantiated, or for splitting the third list, if it is instantiated.

3.5.3. The Algorithm

Below is a summary of the algorithm to generate a set of wait declarations for a single procedure. Wait declarations are represented as sets of arguments that may be constructed.

for-each pair L, of unifiable clause heads and recursive calls **do**
    if the head is as general as the call **then**
        terminate with failure
    else
        for-each argument I, less general in the head **do**
            add a wait declaration to wait group L, with 0 in argument I and 1 in all other arguments
        end-for
    end-if
end-for
Allwaits = {W | W is the intersection of one wait from each group}
Waits = {W | $W \in$ *Allwaits* $\wedge \forall V (V \in$ *Allwaits* $\rightarrow W \not\subset V)$}

This can be implemented simply in PROLOG. An all solutions predicate is very useful for computing *Allwaits*. The performance is reasonable for most inputs, but much more efficient algorithms are possible for large L. For example, [Sagiv 84] investigates the complexity of our algorithm and concludes it can be bettered by adapting an algorithm of theirs.

However, not all complexity arguments are useful in practice. Firstly, mutual recursion in PROLOG is not common, and is very rarely complex. L is usually bounded by the number of rules in the largest recursive procedure, not just the number of rules in the program. Secondly, although the number of different wait groups generated can be as large as 2^a (where a is the arity of the predicate), it rarely exceeds two or three in practice. Even with a large number of recursive rules, only a few different sets of arguments are less general in the clause heads. Thus, the main improvement we can make to the efficiency is to combine some of the L groups of wait declarations, where they are identical (more generally, when one is a subset of another). Our current implementation uses this optimization. Though the complexity of the algorithm is exponential in the size of the input in the worst case, it seems to be linear in practice.

3.5.4. Difficulties With the Algorithm

The algorithm can fail at one point: when a recursive call is being compared with a clause head. If the head is as general as the call, then variables in the call will not be constructed, so the call cannot be delayed by wait declarations. In this case it is worth advising the programmer that some more complex control or logic may be needed at this point.

The algorithm also tends to be too conservative. It makes no assumptions about the default computation rule, though for most rules, some of the infinite loops cannot occur. The result can be wait declarations with more zeros than necessary, or too few wait declarations. Calls which could not cause infinite loops might delay. One reason for this is that some clause heads are more general than they could be. This has lead us to the investigation of *most specific logic programs*, with Jean-Louis Lassez, and the development of an algorithm to make programs as specific as possible [Naish 84b]. Another reason for very general clause heads is the use of PROLOG's representation of integers, rather than zero and the successor function. For example, if the *length* predicate is written using the successor notation, the right wait declarations are found by the algorithm:

    ?– wait length(0, 1).
    ?– wait length(1, 0).
    length([ ], 0).
    length(H.T, s(N)) :– length(T, N).

Below is a program with equivalent logic, using PROLOG's normal representation of integers.

    ?– wait length(0, 1).
    length([ ], 0).
    length(H.T, N) :– N > 0, plus(M, 1, N), length(T, M).

Only the first wait declaration is found by the algorithm, so the program would delay rather than constructing a list of a given length. However, when used in this way, infinite loops could occur if

(1)   the clause order is changed,

(2)   the call to > is left out, or

(3)   *length* is called before >.

Any proof that the program avoids infinite loops must consider the clause selection rule, the computation rule, and the relationship between the constants zero and one, and the predicates > and *plus*. It would be difficult for a program to analyse this, and programmers should be very careful before changing automatically generated wait declarations. Other control or additional tests may be needed to prevent loops.

A further reason why wait declarations sometimes delay calls unnecessarily, is that they deal only with complete arguments. Sometimes a finer granularity is needed. This has been compounded by the treatment of repeated variables in the heads of clauses. Consider the following example.

    ?– wait member(1,0).
    member(A, A.B).
    member(A, B.C) :– member(A, C).

        ← member(1, [X]).

By the definition we gave earlier, the second argument of *member* gets constructed (X gets bound to 1), so the call delays. We really want to delay only calls constructed by the cons, not by B. This kind of behaviour can be avoided as follows.

    ?– wait member(1,0).
    member(A, B.C) :– A=B.
    member(A, B.C) :– member(A, C).

Alternatively, the definition of *constructed* can be changed. Recently, we implemented a slight variant of the original wait declarations, which only delay calls if variables in the call are bound to nonvariables appearing in the head of the clause. In the previous goal, since 1 appeared in the call, and not in the head, the call is not delayed. This is an improvement, but not a general solution. Defining the exact effect of wait declarations is also made more complex. Later, we present a new kind of declaration, which overcomes all these difficulties.

3.5.5. Ordering Subgoals

The behaviour of *length* shows that the order of subgoals can be important, even with extra control information. Here we give some heuristics for reordering subgoals. These are entirely dependent on the default computation rule, which we assume to be depth first and left to right. We also assume there are no nonlogical primitives called. Nonlogical procedures, such as those for doing input and output, cannot be avoided completely, and reordering calls to them is often disastrous.

In the *length* example, it was noted that calling > before *length* prevents an infinite loop. In [Naish 85b], we suggest recursive subgoals should be placed last. Later, we shall propose an alternative to this. A heuristic which is more often useful, is to put *tests* before *generators*. If tests are called first, they can coroutine with generators, often increasing efficiency. Initially, tests are often insufficiently instantiated, so they delay. This allows a generator to start. As soon as a marked variable is bound, some test(s) are resumed and may fail, causing the generator to backtrack. This contrasts with the conventional PROLOG generate and test algorithms, where the generator must produce a complete solution (to the generator) before it is tested. A good example of this is the eight queens problem, given later.

Programmers generally have a good idea of what calls are tests, so they could be relied on for goal ordering. It would be even better to automate the process, though even defining precisely what a test is has not been done previously. General properties are that they are deterministic and, usually, don't construct any variables. However, any call can act as a test in this way, if it is delayed long enough. Conversely, almost all calls can be used to construct variables, if they are called soon enough (in pure PROLOG, at least).

However, some calls usually cause inefficiency or infinite loops if they are used as generators. They act as tests for all efficient forms of control. This leads us to propose the following definition of what a test is.

Definition A subgoal is a *test* if its computation is
a) deterministic and does not construct any variables when it is sufficiently instantiated, and
b) has an infinite number of solutions otherwise.

In other words, it has zero, one or an infinite number of solutions, depending on the instantiation. We also use the term test to denote a procedure for which all possible calls to it are tests. Most of the MU-PROLOG system predicates are tests by this definition. The definition also ties in well with two heuristics we have previously used for recognising user-defined tests using wait declarations, in [Naish 83a] and [Naish 85b].

Our first heuristic was found by observing that most tests had a single wait declaration (with one or more zeros) generated for them. If the wait declarations generated for a procedure prevent a particular argument (or set of arguments) from being constructed, then calls to that procedure must delay until that argument (set) is sufficiently instantiated. This is usually sufficient to avoid non-determinism and constructing variables. The following program illustrates this.

```
?– wait is_list(0).
is_list([ ]).
is_list(M.L) :– list(L).
```

However, preventing some arguments from being constructed does not always ensure determinism. Recall that the second argument of the wait declaration for *member* was zero. If *member* is called with only the second argument instantiated, it can be used as a non-deterministic generator. Our second rule for finding tests recognises this fact. The rule uses the determinism caused by wait declarations in a more precise way.

<u>Definition</u> A procedure is *locally deterministic* if it has at most one matching clause for any (non-delaying) call to it.

By examining the wait declarations and clause heads, we can find which procedures are locally deterministic. This can be used with dependency information (indicating what calls what) to find which calls are completely deterministic. Procedures with one clause are obviously locally deterministic. With more than one clause, we consider each wait declaration and check that only one clause can be matched if the procedure is called in that way. This is true if the arguments in the clause heads corresponding to zeros in the wait declaration cannot all be unified. For example, [ ] and M.L do not unify, so *is_list* is locally deterministic, whereas A.B and B1.C unify, so *member* can be non-deterministic. The successor version of *length* is also shown to be deterministic. For the first declaration, [ ] and H.T do not unify and for the second declaration, 0 and s(N) do not unify.

Length is not actually a test by our definition, since it constructs variables. It can even be used in multiple ways. There are two ways to deal with this. The first is to ignore it and treat *length* as a test anyway. This is reasonable, since it is desirable to do deterministic calls before non-deterministic calls anyway (we discuss this more later). A second possibility is to use our first heuristic as a secondary method for ordering calls. Calls which are deterministic and never construct particular arguments are most likely to be tests. These should be placed first, followed by other deterministic calls, followed by other non-constructing calls then other non-deterministic calls. This method is used in our current implementation of the preprocessor, which we discuss next.

3.6. A Program to Generate Control Information

We will now describe a preprocessor for logic programs, which we have developed. The program will input the logic of a problem (which can be considered a specification) and outputs a program with equivalent logic and control information to aid efficiency and termination. Comments are also produced, to show the results of analysis, what changes are made and where the preprocessor was unable to generate control information (so a programmer can intervene). To illustrate its behaviour, we shall use the following eight queens program as an example.

```
queen(X) :- perm(1.2.3.4.5.6.7.8.[ ], X), safe(X).

perm([ ], [ ]).
perm(X.Y, U.V) :- perm(Z, V), delete(U, X.Y, Z).

delete(A, A.L, L).
delete(X, A.B.L, A.R) :- delete(X, B.L, R).

safe([ ]).
safe(N.L) :- safe(L), nodiag(N, 1, L).

nodiag(_, _, [ ]).
nodiag(B, D, N.L) :-
          D =\= N-B, D =\= B-N,
          D1 is D + 1, nodiag(B, D1, L).
```

The preprocessor currently has three passes, each storing information used by later passes and/or generating control information. The first pass reads the input, stores it and initializes some book-keeping information. During this pass a graph is constructed, indicating which procedures call which other procedures. This is used to detect recursion, for generating wait declarations, and for finding deterministic and nonlogical procedures.

In the next pass each procedure is analysed and control primitives are added (currently, only wait declarations are produced). The analysis also reveals which procedures should be used as tests. We have described, in general terms, how to recognise database and recursive procedures, and add control information to them. This can be extended to other types of procedures for which control can be automated. A further extension is to split procedures and make other transformations which result in equivalent logic, but facilitate the generation of control information. If a procedure is not a recognisable type, a message should printed, indicating that programmer assistance is desirable. Currently, the preprocessor warns of a possible infinite loop when it cannot generate wait declarations for a procedure.

In the eight queens example, the *queen* predicate needs no control primitives, but all the others are recognised as recursive procedures. The following wait declarations are generated, using the algorithm described previously. These declarations eliminate all sources of nondeterminism except calls to *delete*.

```
?- wait perm(1, 0).
?- wait perm(0, 1).
?- wait delete(1, 1, 0).
?- wait delete(1, 0, 1).
?- wait safe(0).
?- wait nodiag(1, 1, 0).
```

The final pass adjusts the order of calls in each clause that does not call nonlogical procedures. Tests are put at the start, using the ordering discussed earlier. Recursive calls and calls to procedures for which wait declarations could not be generated are placed last. The reordered program, complete with control information, is then output. *Safe* and *nodiag* are recognised as tests by both our heuristics. *Perm* is locally deterministic, but since it calls *delete*, it is not considered to be a test.

The precise output from preprocessing the eight queens program is as follows:

```
% output from logic preprocessor
%
% procedure queen/1 is locally deterministic
% procedure perm/2 is locally deterministic
% procedure safe/1 doesnt construct some arg(s)
% procedure safe/1 is locally deterministic
% procedure nodiag/3 doesnt construct some arg(s)
% procedure nodiag/3 is locally deterministic
% procedure safe/1 is deterministic
% procedure nodiag/3 is deterministic
% clause altered: queen(X) :- . . .
% clause altered: perm(X.Y, U.V) :- . . .
% clause altered: safe(N.L) :- . . .


queen(X) :-
        safe(X),
        perm(1.2.3.4.5.6.7.8.[ ], X).


?- wait perm(1, 0).
?- wait perm(0, 1).
perm([ ], [ ]).
perm(X.Y, U.V) :-
        delete(U, X.Y, Z),
        perm(Z, V).


?- wait delete(1, 1, 0).
?- wait delete(1, 0, 1).
delete(A, A.L, L).
delete(X, A.B.L, A.R) :-
        delete(X, B.L, R).


?- wait safe(0).
safe([ ]).
safe(N.L) :-
        nodiag(N, 1, L),
        safe(L).


?- wait nodiag(1, 1, 0).
nodiag(_, _, [ ]).
nodiag(B, D, N.L) :-
        D =\= N - B,
        D =\= B - N,
        D1 is D + 1,
        nodiag(B, D1, L).
```

To solve the eight queens problem with this program, the following goal would normally be used:

← queen(X).

The preprocessor finds the three pieces of control information necessary to make this goal execute efficiently:

(1)   *Safe* is called before *perm*. This makes the tests delay initially, so they can act as coroutines, waking whenever *perm* further instantiates the list of queen positions.

(2)   *Safe* has a zero wait declaration, to stop it from attempting to guess the length of the list. This would be inefficient and would lead to an infinite loop if all solutions were sought.

(3)   *Nodiag* also has a wait declaration, with the last argument zero, for the same reasons.

Perm generates the list of queen positions, and coroutines with the *safe* and *nodiag* tests. After the positions of the first N queens have been decided, there is one call to *safe* delayed, and N calls to *nodiag* delayed (one for each queen). When a new queen is added, these calls are woken. Each of the calls to *nodiag* checks if the new queen can be taken. The call to *safe* creates a call to *nodiag*, for the new queen, and another call to *safe*. When all eight queens have been successfully placed, *perm* binds the end of the list to [ ] and all the delayed calls succeed.

Because *perm* constructs the list X before the next queen position is chosen (by *delete*), there is some unnecessary delaying of calls. This does not affect the order of efficiency, however, and can be avoided if the program is slightly altered. Thus, in this case, the preprocessor is able to make the program run efficiently. Even when programmer intervention is needed, it helps considerably, by providing some control information, as well as comments.

A final point about this example is that the problems with *perm* discussed in [Elcock 83] are also solved. In most PROLOG systems, *perm* causes an infinite loop if the arguments to the initial call are swapped. It is actually quite difficult to write a version of *perm* which works either way in conventional PROLOGs. The most widely used version of *perm*, in the DEC-10 PROLOG/C-PROLOG library, only works if the first argument in instantiated (despite documentation to the contrary). In MU-PROLOG, the wait declarations generated for *delete* prevent the infinite loops, so *perm* can be used either way.

3.7. Further Examples

The examples we have given so far illustrate the use of control for database procedures (*stud_unit* etc.), and for some styles of recursive programming. Included were multi-use procedures (*append3*, *length* and *perm*), and generate and test procedures (*queen*). We now give further examples of the use of automatically generated control with other styles of programming.

3.7.1. Systems Programming

The following example shows how useful delaying can be in certain systems programming tasks. The delaying of various built-in predicates is particularly important. The task is to write a term comparison predicate, for sorting answers in our all solutions predicate, among other things.

Given two terms, the predicate should return =, < or >. The standard term ordering is integers (from lowest to highest) then other terms ordered first on arity (constants have arity zero) then name (in lexicographic order) and each argument (from left to right).

The system predicates our implementation uses are ~=, *int*, <, =.., *length*, and *name*. Because all these predicates delay when insufficiently instantiated, *term_compare* can be written in quite a straightforward way. The logic was fairly simple to get right, but during testing, a complex goal apparently caused the program to loop. Finding and preventing such a loop, by conventional means, can be time consuming and difficult. Without some delaying mechanism, it is probably impossible. However, our first reaction was not even to try to look for the bug. Instead, we ran the program through the preprocessor, with the following result.

```
term_compare((=), X, X).
term_compare(C, X, Y) :- X ~= Y, compare1(X, Y, C).

compare1(X, Y, (<)) :- int(X), int(Y), X < Y.
compare1(X, Y, (>)) :- int(X), int(Y), X > Y.
compare1(X, Y, (<)) :- int(X), non_int(Y).
compare1(X, Y, (>)) :- int(Y), non_int(X).
compare1(X, Y, C) :- X =.. XF.XA, Y =.. YF.YA,
        length(XA, XN), length(YA, YN),
        (       XN < YN, C = (<)
        ;       XN > YN, C = (>)
        ;       XN = YN, ncompare(XF, XA, YF, YA, C)).

ncompare(XF, XA, XF, YA, C) :- lcompare(XA, YA, C).
ncompare(XF, XA, YF, YA, C) :- XF ~= YF,
        name(XF, XN), name(YF, YN), scompare(XN, YN, C).

?- wait lcompare(1, 0, 1).
?- wait lcompare(0, 1, 1).
lcompare(A.XA, B.YA, C) :- term_compare(C1, A, B),
        (       C1 = (<), C = (<)
        ;       C1 = (>), C = (>)
        ;       C1 = (=), lcompare(XA, YA, C)).

?- wait scompare(1, 0, 1).
?- wait scompare(0, 1, 1).
scompare([], [], (=)).
scompare([], _._, (<)).
scompare(_._, [], (>)).
scompare(A.X, A.Y, C) :- scompare(X, Y, C).
scompare(A.X, B.Y, (<)) :- A < B.
scompare(A.X, B.Y, (>)) :- A > B.

non_int(X) :- X =.. _.
```

As expected, the program then worked correctly. In fact, we still do not know what caused the loop, or if all the generated wait declarations are actually necessary. The operational behaviour of this program is undoubtably horrendous, but we were able to write it entirely declaratively. For our all solutions predicate we made just one slight alteration, to stop some backtracking when the terms are insufficiently instantiated. *Term_compare* should probably be written in C in the MU-PROLOG interpreter, but for a compiler based system or rapid prototyping, our MU-PROLOG version is adequate.

3.7.2. Object Oriented Programming

Investigation of Concurrent Prolog [Shapiro 83a] has lead to an interest in an object oriented style of programming in logic programming languages [Shapiro 83b]. Objects correspond to procedure calls, clauses specify state transitions of objects and messages are passed by instantiating streams (lists) shared by two or more objects. The main features of Concurrent Prolog that enable this, are and-parallelism and read only variable annotations.

And-parallelism can easily be simulated by coroutining and wait declarations can be used to provide the same control as read only variables in nearly all cases. In all published Concurrent Prolog programs we know of, wait declarations can replace read only annotations very simply. In fact, control in the object oriented style of programming is nearly always just waiting for a stream to become further instantiated. Our algorithm for generating wait declarations copes very well with this. The following program is based on an example from [Shapiro 83a]. A stack object is used to check if a list of parentheses and braces is balanced.

```
balanced :- instream(I, balanced(I)).

balanced(X) :- stack(Y), balanced(X, Y).

?- wait balanced(1, 0).
?- wait balanced(0, 1).
balanced(40.X, push('(').Y) :- balanced(X, Y).
balanced(123.X, push('{').Y) :- balanced(X, Y).
balanced(41.X, pop('(').Y) :- balanced(X, Y).
balanced(125.X, pop('{').Y) :- balanced(X, Y).
balanced([ ], [ ]).

stack(S) :- stack(S, [ ]).

?- wait stack(0, 1).
stack(pop(X).S, X.Xs) :- stack(S, Xs).
stack(push(X).S, Xs) :- stack(S, X.Xs).
stack([ ], [ ]).

?- consult(instream).
```

The *balanced*/1 predicate creates a stack object and a *balanced*/2 object. The *balanced* object receives messages in the form of ASCII character codes for parentheses and braces and sends push and pop messages to the *stack* object. The computation succeeds if the stack is empty at the end of the input. The wait declarations force both procedures to delay until their input streams are sufficiently instantiated. The behaviour is identical to the Concurrent Prolog version, but the control is added automatically.

The call to *instream* binds I to the input stream of characters typed at the terminal and calls *balanced*. I is instantiated incrementally, as each character is typed, allowing concurrent input and processing. Most of the time, the calls to *stack* and *balanced* are delayed, and the MU-PROLOG process is waiting. When a character is typed, the process receives an interrupt and is resumed. I is then instantiated, waking *balanced* which, in turn, wakes *stack*. *Instream* also handles backtracking correctly, though it is not needed in this particular example. It is partly written in C, using the dynamic loading facilities of MU-PROLOG.

The next example shows how even with quite a complicated arrangement of streams, the control is still fairly simple. It is an insertion sort with a separate object for each integer, in the style of some CSP programs. Associated with each object is an integer and four streams. Two of the streams are used to pass new elements to be inserted from the object on the left and to the object on the right. The other two streams are used for returning answers, from right to left, when the input stream has ended. The right-most object acts as a sentinel.

```
sort(A, B) :- maxint(M), Min is -M-1,
        sort1(Min, A, _, [], Min.B).
```

```
?- wait sort1(1, 0, 1, 1, 1).
sort1(N, [], [], P_out, N.P_out).
sort1(N, N1.P_in, N1.S_in, P_out, S_out) :- N1 =< N,
        sort1(N, P_in, S_in, P_out, S_out).
sort1(N, N1.P_in, S_in, P_out, S_out) :- N1 > N,
        sort1(N1, P_in, N_in, P_out, N_out),
        sort1(N, N_in, S_in, N_out, S_out).
```

Two features of Concurrent Prolog that are not easily implemented in MU-PROLOG are "don't care nondeterminism" (the commit operator) and or-parallelism. PROLOG uses don't know nondeterminism, implemented by backtracking. One advantage of this is that when the inference system terminates, it is complete (so negation as failure can be used). The cut primitive can be used for don't care nondeterminism, though great care must be taken, especially with coroutines. The need for or-parallelism can also be eliminated, in many cases, by making the conditions for delaying stronger.

We are currently working on automatically translating a language like Flat Concurrent Prolog into MU-PROLOG. The delaying primitive used is wait declarations and there are restrictions on the complexity of the guards. Below is a (hand) translation of the standard *merge* procedure, perhaps the most common use of don't care nondeterminism.

```
?- wait merge(0, 0, 1).
merge(xxxx, xxxx, _) :- fail.
merge(L, N, A.M) :- nonvar(L), L = A.L1, !, merge(L1, N, M).
merge(L, N, A.M) :- nonvar(N), N = A.N1, !, merge(L, N1, M).
merge(L, N, N) :- nonvar(L), L = [], !.
merge(N, L, N) :- nonvar(L), L = [].
```

The wait declaration and first clause ensure *merge* delays until at least one guard can succeed completely. The extra *nonvar* and = tests ensure the correct clause is chosen, and the cuts replace commits to force determinism. This version of *merge* is currently being used in an implementation of an object oriented programming language at Melbourne University by Richard Helm. The use of MU-PROLOG as a target language for compiling a parallel-style logic programming language will be the subject of a future report.

3.7.3. Infinite Streams

Automatic control can also be useful for programs that use infinite streams, though MU-PROLOG is not the ideal language for this. Firstly, the memory management is very simple and inadequate for large examples. Secondly, the computation is not demand driven, so constructing infinite streams which are not used in the rest of the computation is difficult to avoid. Finally, the output primitives of MU-PROLOG are not very well suited to infinite streams. It is often easy to write a program that will compute a stream successfully, but printing the stream can be difficult. Below is a program which implements the sieve of Eratosthenes algorithm, for computing prime numbers, as output from the preprocessor.

```
primes :- writelist(X), sift(2.Y, X), ints(2.Y).

?- wait writelist(0).
writelist(N.L) :- writeln(N), writelist(L).

ints(N.X) :- plus(N, 1, N1), X = N1.Y, ints(N1.Y).

?- wait sift(1, 0).
?- wait sift(0, 1).
sift(X.Y, X.Z) :- filter(X, Y, A), sift(A, Z).

?- wait filter(1, 0, 1).
filter(X, Y.Z, A) :- Y mod X =\= 0, A = Y.B, filter(X, Z, B).
filter(X, Y.Z, A) :- Y mod X =:= 0, filter(X, Z, A).
```

The initial call to *primes* creates three "processes", to write the list of primes, create the list of primes and create a list of integers. *Sift* creates a *filter* process for each prime. To be able to print the list of primes it was necessary to make two small changes to the simplest logic. In the clauses for *ints* and *filter*, a cons in the head of the clause was replaced by a variable and a call to = was added to the body. This ensures that *writelist* is called only when the first element of the list is instantiated to the next prime. Without this, *writelist* can write uninstantiated variables and can be affected by backtracking.

Changing the *ints* clause also affects the control that is generated. With the program above, the preprocessor produces a warning that *ints* may cause an infinite loop. In this case, an infinite loop is precisely what we want. With a less general clause head instead of the equality, however, the preprocessor produces a wait declaration for *ints* which stops the loop. Instead of printing a list of primes, the program just terminates with a few calls still delayed. With programs that use infinite streams in MU-PROLOG, there is usually a specific process that acts as a generator of an infinite list. Sometimes the code has to be changed slightly to stop the preprocessor from adding wait declarations to prevent this, but the control on other procedures rarely require intervention. An alternative, which we discuss later, is to allow calls delayed by wait declarations to proceed if there are no other calls to do.

3.8. Related Work

3.8.1. PROLOG M

PROLOG M [Babb 83] uses a rule for delaying system predicates which is very similar to the heuristic on which our wait declaration algorithm is based. Consider the following PROLOG M program.

append(A, B, C) <-> A=[ ] and B=C
　　　　　　　　or A=D.E and C=D.F and append(E, B, F).

PROLOG M does not use unification in the heads of clauses but has an = system predicate which implements a restricted form of unification. All systems predicates delay when they have an infinite number of solutions, so if B and C are variables, B=C delays rather than binding one variable to the other. If user-defined procedures are written with recursive subgoals last, calls to them with infinite numbers of solutions often result in delaying. [Babb 83] gives the following example of such a goal.

← append(X, [2], Y).

However, there is a subtle but important distinction between the behaviour of MU-PROLOG and PROLOG M in examples such as this. In MU-PROLOG (with automatically generated wait declarations), the initial call delays immediately. In PROLOG M, some computation takes place first. One solution is found from the first part of the disjunction, with X=[] and Y=[2]. In the execution of the second part of the disjunction, the two calls to = delay and the recursive call to append succeeds (with E=[ ] and F=[2]). The calls to = remain delayed but the recursive call creates a choice point. On backtracking, another choice point is created before the computation delays. This causes an infinite loop in the following goal.

← append(X, [2], Y), fail.

Though the control in PROLOG M is based on a heuristic very similar to ours, it is only implemented effectively in system predicates. User-defined predicates tend to delay one choice point too late. This makes the control much less effective.

3.8.2. Data Flow Analysis

Several people have attacked control and related problems in logic programming by analysing the flow of data from one call to the next, via shared variables. On the surface, the work on inverting programs [Sickel 79] is very similar to ours. An algorithm is given for producing declarations containing ones and zeros. However, they are used to find what arguments will be completely instantiated by the program, assuming it terminates. In our work, making the program terminate is important, and whether arguments are fully instantiated is of no concern. The algorithm for generating DEC-10 PROLOG mode declarations [Mellish 81] also has a quite different purpose. It assumes a left to right computation rule, rather than providing information for alternative computation rules.

[Reddy 85] investigates some relationships between logic and functional programming. In functional languages, the control is built into the program implicitly. Logic programming can allow different control, depending on which arguments of a procedure call are instantiated. Reddy introduces a type of mode declaration, to make control fixed, as in functional languages. Some rules are given for determining allowable modes, but these are not always sufficient for eliminating all poor choices of control. For example, in the following reverse program, a verbal argument is needed to justify why *reverse* should proceed ahead of *append* when *reverse* is called with its first argument instantiated.

reverse([ ], [ ]).
reverse(A.B, C) :– reverse(B, D), append(D, [A], C).

[Bellia 83] uses similar rules for finding allowable modes and ordering calls for demand driven execution. This scheme can also generate multiple possible modings in programs like *reverse*. Our algorithm could often be used to find the best one. It does so in this example.

3.8.3. Capture Rules

Capture rules are also based mainly on data flow analysis but the amount of work and relevance to ours warrants a separate section. Capture rules were originally introduced in [Ullman 84], for planning query evaluation in function-free deductive databases with recursive rules. [Sagiv 84] investigated ways in which they could be extended, to provide control like our *merge* example. More work was needed to handle functions and find that *merge* could be used for splitting lists, as well as merging them. Complexity of the algorithms was also investigated. [Ullman 85] provides further extensions by analysing inequalities in argument sizes. This is really the essence of our algorithm.

Capture rules rest on a firmer theoretical base than our algorithm. They have the advantage that if they can be applied, the subsequent computation is guaranteed to terminate. However, it also means that they can be applied less often. The normal definitions of naive reverse and merge sort had to be slightly modified in [Ullman 85] for the capture rules to be applied. With further work, this may not be necessary so often. Another limitation of capture rules is that they deal rigorously only with termination. Efficiency is still a matter for heuristics, and more complex methods of proving termination may not help. Also, a much simpler solution, to just the termination problem, is to use a fair computation rule. Unfortunately, attacking the efficiency problem directly seems very difficult. We discuss these issues more later.

3.9. Other Control Primitives

In this section we deal with alternatives to wait declarations (most alternatives to priority declarations are fairly similar). A major factor in the comparisons we give is whether the control primitives can be generated automatically, by modifying the algorithm given to generate wait declarations, for example. First, control which is local to single calls is discussed, followed by the more difficult area of non-local control.

3.9.1. Local Control

A primitive similar to the *key* facility in ABSYS [Foster 69] has been suggested in [Warren 79], called *triggers*. *Triggers* are similar to wait declarations, but they cause delays if arguments in the call are variables, rather than if the arguments get constructed. They are simpler than wait declarations, since their effect is independent of the clause heads and unification algorithm, and calls cannot succeed with the first clause and delay when other clauses are tried. This is significant from a theoretical point of view, as we shall see. *Triggers* can be generated and used in the same way as wait declarations in many cases, but not all, as the following example illustrates.

    ordered([ ]).
    ordered([A]).
    ordered(A.B.C) :– A =< B, ordered(B.C).

Triggers cannot delay the recursive call to *ordered* since its argument is never a variable (though it may be constructed, causing an infinite loop). Such cases are not uncommon and we consider that this outweighs the advantages of *triggers*. It is possible to combine most of the advantages of waits and *triggers* by allowing more complex terms in the declarations, rather than just zeros and ones. A more complex algorithm is needed to determine if a call delays, so interpreting these declarations would be slower. However, they could be implemented efficiently in a compiler-based system. For the next implementation of PROLOG at Melbourne University, currently being written by J. Schultz, we have suggested *when declarations* as the control primitive.

    ?– merge(A, B, C) when A and B or C.
    ?– ordered(A.B) when B.

The first declaration states that *merge* can be called if the first two arguments, or the last argument, are non-variables. The second declaration says to call *ordered* when the argument is not a cons, or it is a cons with a nonvariable second argument. Multiple when declarations are also allowed, though they are not needed so often because the bodies can contain disjunctions. These examples show how when declarations can provide similar control to wait declarations. In fact, they are more flexible, since different parts within single arguments can be distinguished. This is useful for procedures such as *member*. We have recently completed a simple prototype compiler for when declarations.

Control information attached to calls was mentioned in Section 3.3.2 and we now discuss it further. The simplest primitive of this kind is the *geler* (freeze) predicate of PROLOG-II [Colmerauer 82]. An example of its use is:

    ordered([ ]).
    ordered([A]).
    ordered(A.B.C) :– A =< B, freeze(C, ordered(B.C)).

The effect of *freeze* here is to delay the recursive call to *ordered* until C is a non-variable. When called with a variable as its argument, this version of *ordered* makes two "guesses" at the length of the list and then delays, avoiding further inefficiency, and a possible infinite loop.

The wait declaration algorithm can be modified to produce control attached to calls, if there is a primitive that will delay calls until any one of several arguments is sufficiently instantiated. *Freeze* only waits for one variable to be bound and cannot easily provide the control we used for *append*, *merge* or *delete*. It seems useful to extend *freeze*, so it accepts a list, and delays until at least one member is a non-variable. This can be implemented (with one slight problem) using *freeze*. As an illustration, we give an implementation of a version of *freeze* that waits until either of two variables becomes bound.

```
        % calls P when X or Y become bound
freeze2(X, Y, P) :-
        freeze(X, once(Called, P)),
        freeze(Y, once(Called, P)).


        % This stops P (as above) from being called twice
once(Called, P) :-
        var(Called),       % if P not called already then
        call(P),           %      call P
        Called = true.     %      Called = true
once(Called, P) :-
        nonvar(Called).    % else succeed
```

As can be seen, we need to be a bit tricky to stop P being called twice, if both variables are eventually instantiated. Also, if one variable never becomes instantiated, one of the calls to *freeze* will never be woken. Obviously, a lower level implementation would be better in all respects.

Like *triggers*, even an extended form of *freeze* can not provide adequate control in some cases where clause heads have more than one level of functor. For example, the following program and goal cause an infinite loop which cannot be avoided just by using *freeze* for calls to *even* (with MU-PROLOG, the calls to *even* delay and the subsequent computation may fail).

```
even(0).
even(s(s(N))) :- even(N).

    ← even(X), even(Y), Y = s(X), . . .
```

3.9.2. Non-local Control

Non-local control is generally more expensive to implement than local control, since more information is needed to determine whether a call delays. Typically, the ancestors of the call may need to be examined. We believe that forms of non-local control should be devised specifically for the areas where local control is insufficient and, if possible, with automation in mind. IC-PROLOG's *lazy producers* provide the type of control needed for multiple generators to act as coroutines. It may be possible to generate this control information automatically, using similar analysis to ours. Where clause heads are as general as recursive calls (so wait declarations have no effect) it can be useful to have control primitives which will examine the ancestors of the call, to try to avoid infinite loops. In practice, most infinite loops in PROLOG are quite simple, so the undecidability of the halting problem does not imply such control is futile.

There have been some forms of control suggested which do not merely affect the computation rule. Altering the clause selection rule is one example [Gallaire 80]. This control is really beyond the scope of this thesis. Also, if the control is abused, the correctness of programs can be affected, so extra knowledge about the program or problem domain is necessary for the safe use of this control. If a lot of analysis and knowledge are needed to generate control information, then it may be feasible to use the knowledge for program transformation instead. Advantages of this are that simpler control is needed at run-time and it is easier to extend the language to include a larger subset of first order logic.

3.10. Summary

In conventional PROLOG, simple, lucid programs often lead to inefficient algorithms and infinite loops. Efficiency can only be achieved by transforming the logic of the program. There are now several systems in which the same result can often be achieved more easily, simply by adding control information. We believe the next stage of development is the automation of control. A further step is to automate program transformation. There will always be a use for experts, who know or can invent clever algorithms, but this does not detract from the usefulness of such systems. Even for expert programmers, automated control is often very valuable. Also, for runnable specifications, once-off programs, and programs written by inexperienced users, ease of writing is far more important than efficiency of execution.

The system we have described in this chapter is a first step towards automation of control and the results obtained so far have been encouraging. We have shown conclusively that this approach can be rewarding, and have made some important advances. Priority declarations are an extension to a proven method of control for database procedures, and the precise way in which they are used is flexible and can take into account factors such as indexing. We have found wait declarations to be a simple and effective form of control for recursive procedures. When declarations promise to be even better, especially for a compiler-based system.

4. HETEROGENEOUS SLD RESOLUTION

4.1. Introduction

The growing interest in logic programming has prompted the theoretical investigation of SLD resolution. Of particular importance is the work on soundness and completeness, for success and finite failure (for example, [Hill 74], [Clark 83b], [Apt 82], [Lloyd 84b] and [Wolfram 84]). Two key results are that SLD resolution is sound and complete, for any computation rule. Capitalizing on this, several systems have been implemented which allow flexible computation rules. However, the lack of a rigorous definition of what a computation rule is, has lead to a discrepancy between theory and practice.

For a particular goal clause, the current theory allows the computation rule to select any one atom. Each clause with a head that unifies with the selected atom leads to a child goal clause. In most implementations, these children are examined sequentially, using backtracking. However, in some systems (such as MU-PROLOG and IC-PROLOG), after one child has been examined, the original goal clause can be re-examined and another atom selected. In general, the children are determined by a sequence of selected atoms, rather a single one (hence the name, Heterogeneous SLD resolution). The number of possible sequences depends on the size of the goal and the number of matching clauses. Even with one matching clause per atom, and N atoms, there are over N! possible choices. The current theory only allows for N possibilities.

Heterogeneous SLD (HSLD) resolution is not restricted to modelling current systems. To illustrate this, Section 4.4 describes a computation rule which implements a form of intelligent backtracking and can interact favourably with other rules. First, though, HSLD resolution is precisely defined and some theoretical results are proved.

4.2. Definitions

For comparison, we first give definitions used in standard SLD resolution. Corresponding definitions are then given for HSLD resolution.

4.2.1. SLD Resolution

Given a program P (a set of Horn Clauses) and a goal G (a negative clause), an *SLD tree* for P $\cup$ {G} is defined as follows:

- Each node in the tree is a goal plus a substitution, the root being G plus the empty substitution.
- Each non-empty goal contains a *selected* atom.
- If the goal is $G_1,..,G_i,..,G_j$, the selected atom is G_i, and the substitution is θ, then the node has a child for each clause in P whose head unifies with $G_i\theta$.
- If the clause (variant) is $H \leftarrow B_1,..,B_k$, and γ is a most general unifier of H and $G_i\theta$, then the child node is the goal $G_1,..,G_{i-1},B_1,..,B_k,G_{i+1},..,G_j$, plus the composition of the substitutions θ and γ. $B_1,..,B_k$ are called the *introduced atoms*.

- Variables in the clauses are renamed, so they do not appear in any previous goal.

This definition is slightly unorthodox, in that the goals and substitutions are separated. In most other definitions, a substitution is applied to each child goal, which obscures the connections with atoms in the parent goal. Our definition simplifies the theory (for example, our fairness condition in Section 4.3) and also reflects most implementations more closely.

SLD branches that end in the empty goal as called *success branches*. Other finite branches are called *failure branches*. For each atom in an SLD branch, its *selected clause* is the clause whose head it is (eventually) unified with. Two SLD branches are called *similar* if they have the same initial goal and contain the same atoms and selected clauses (possibly in a different order). The *answer substitution* of a success branch, is the subset of the final substitution which applies to variables in the initial goal. The function that determines the selected atoms is called the *computation rule*. The computation rule does not affect the number or length of success branches, but markedly affects the size of the tree. This has important consequences for the design of efficient SLD refutation procedures.

SLD resolution is the nondeterministic construction of an SLD success branch for the program and goal. In practice, the nondeterminism is achieved by searching. However, due to the "independence" of the computation rule, not all combinations of selected atoms and clauses need to be considered. Atom selection is a case of don't care nondeterminism, so only one SLD tree needs to be searched to find all solutions. Heuristics can be used to attempt to find a small tree to search.

4.2.2. HSLD Resolution

HSLD resolution offers a more flexible way of avoiding the cost of searching all possible combinations of selected atoms and clauses: only one HSLD tree needs to be searched. There are far more HSLD trees to choose from, and the smallest one can be smaller than the smallest SLD tree. There are also more opportunities for introducing heuristics to find a small tree.

HSLD trees are similar to SLD trees, but the nodes contain more information. Associated with each atom in the tree is a *clause set*, made up of program clauses that *match* the atom (that is, the heads of the clauses unify with the atom after the substitution has been made). To simplify this definition, we impose an order on the children of each node (this does not constrain the way in which the tree is searched).

- Each node is a goal, plus a clause set for each atom in that goal, plus a substitution.
- In the root goal, G, clause sets for the atoms contain all matching clauses, and the substitution is the empty substitution.
- For each non-empty goal, the computation rule selects a sequence of atom–clause pairs. The atom is selected from the goal, and the clause is selected from the atom's clause set.
- All clauses in at least one clause set must be selected.
- The atoms and substitutions in each child are the same as in SLD trees.
- The clause sets of introduced atoms contain all matching clauses.
- The other clause sets in the child contain the clauses from the parent which still match,

and have not been selected for any previous sibling.

Definitions of success branches, etc., are all extended in the obvious way. For an example of an HSLD tree, consider the following program and goal:

```
p(Y) :- q(a).        q(d).
p(a).                q(e).
p(b).
p(c).
```

← p(X), q(X).

The root contains ←p(X){p(Y):-q(a) ; p(a) ; p(b) ; p(c)}, q(X){q(d) ; q(e)}.
The example below illustrates a possible computation rule. It shows the sequence of selected atom–clause pairs, and the corresponding children (after the substitutions are applied). The HSLD tree is shown in Figure 4.1.

Atom	Clause	Child
p(X)	p(Y):-q(a)	←q(a){}, q(X){q(d) ; q(e)}
q(X)	q(d)	←p(d){}
q(X)	q(e)	←p(e){}

At this point, everything in the clause set of q(X) has been selected, so no more children are needed. Note that the clause sets for the last two children do not contain p(Y):-q(a), since that clause was selected for the first child. This behaviour can be achieved in MU-PROLOG, by having a zero wait declaration for procedure p, and in IC-PROLOG, by making the call to p an eager consumer of X.

The example also illustrates how HSLD resolution can lead to a smaller search space than SLD resolution. This can be surprising, initially, since all clauses in at least one set must be selected at each stage. The reason is that SLD trees may contain several instances of the same failed sub-tree, which can be factored out in HSLD trees. In the example above, q(a) is shown to fail once, rather than once for each solution to q(X). The optimal SLD trees for the goal above have five nodes, compared with four, for HSLD trees (see Figure 4.1).

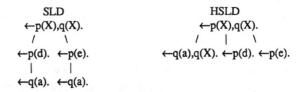

Figure 4.1.

4.3. Theoretical Results

In [Wolfram 84] appears the most concise proof to date of the soundness and completeness of SLD resolution, with respect to success and finite failure (finite failure completeness is subject to a fairness condition). In fact, the results are proved for another extension of SLD resolution. The various characterizations of these results are not discussed here. We just show that the same results apply to HSLD resolution also.

The soundness of HSLD resolution is a direct consequence of the soundness of SLD resolution, since HSLD branches are, in essence, no different from SLD branches. We now define the fairness condition, simplified from [Lassez 84], then give a theorem from which the other results follow.

Definition An SLD (HSLD) branch is *fair* if it is failed or every atom in it is eventually selected. *Fair HSLD resolution* is HSLD resolution restricted to fair branches.

Theorem For all pairs of SLD and HSLD trees of $P \cup \{G\}$,
if there exists a success (fair infinite) branch in the HSLD tree, then there exists a similar success (infinite) branch in the SLD tree and
if there exists a success (fair infinite) branch in the SLD tree, then there exists a similar success (infinite) branch in the HSLD tree.

Proof If there is an HSLD success (fair infinite) branch then at least one SLD tree with a similar success (fair infinite) branch can be found by choosing a computation rule which selects the same atoms in that branch. Therefore, all SLD trees have a similar success (infinite) branch. This is proved in [Wolfram 84]. For success branches, it is a consequence of SLD soundness and strong completeness.

To prove the other half of the theorem, we present an algorithm to find a similar success (infinite) HSLD branch, given a success (fair infinite) SLD branch:

> **while** the HSLD root goal is not empty **do**
>> {*Invariant: All atoms in the root of the HSLD tree are in the SLD branch, and the clause sets contain all selected clauses for the respective atoms in the SLD branch.*}
>>
>> Choose the first child of the root of the HSLD tree which is derived by selecting an atom–clause pair also used somewhere in the SLD branch.
>>
>> {*This must exist, since all clauses in at least one set are selected and all atoms in the SLD branch are selected eventually.*}
>>
>> Now consider the HSLD (sub)tree with this node at the root.
>
> **end**

For success branches, the algorithm must terminate (since no extraneous atoms are introduced) and find a similar branch. Conversely, if the algorithm terminates, then the SLD branch must be finite. Therefore, if the SLD branch is infinite, then the algorithm does not terminate but there is an infinite HSLD branch. □

Corollary HSLD resolution is complete with respect to success.

Proof SLD resolution is complete and if there is an SLD success branch, then there is a similar HSLD success branch, with an equivalent answer substitution, in all HSLD trees. □

Corollary HSLD resolution is sound with respect to finite failure.

Proof If an HSLD tree is finitely failed, then it has no success or infinite branches, so no fair SLD trees have success or infinite branches. Hence, by the (finite failure) soundness of SLD resolution, so is HSLD resolution. □

Corollary Fair HSLD resolution is complete with respect to finite failure.

Proof If an SLD tree is finitely failed, then no fair HSLD tree has a success or infinite branch. □

4.4. An Application

HSLD resolution was initially conceived to make the theoretical basis of MU-PROLOG (and similar systems) more rigorous. A side effect has been an understanding of the greater flexibility possible for refutation procedures. In this section we describe a computation rule for HSLD resolution which can be viewed in several ways. It is first described informally, using different viewpoints, then a more formal definition is given.

To minimize the size of the search tree, computation rules should tend to select atoms that fail. The following variant of the killer heuristic (used for searching game trees) can be used to this effect. If an atom is found to fail when selected at one node of an HSLD tree, it is likely to fail if selected at the parent node. This can easily be incorporated into a computation rule, by taking account of a previous failure when the next atom is selected.

This rule can also be seen as a form of intelligent backtracking. When a failure occurs in an intelligent backtracking system, an analysis reveals where the failure originated, and the system backtracks to that point. This can avoid many other choices which would inevitably lead to failure. The analysis requires various data which must be stored during forward execution (see [Bruynooghe 83], for example). A simpler way to detect where the failure originated is to backtrack one step at a time, retrying the failed goal at each stage. Forward execution should be less expensive, since no extra information need be stored, though backtracking over a large number of choice points would be slower.

More formally, the first atom selected at a node is determined by some default rule (depth first, left to right, for example). For subsequent choices, if an atom in a child is found to fail and it occurs in the goal, then it is selected, otherwise the previous atom selection is repeated. The selections continue until one of the clause sets has been exhausted. The following example illustrates some features of such a computation rule:

```
p(X) :- q(X).        q(d).
p(b).                q(e).
p(c).

      ← p(X), q(a).
```

The computation proceeds as follows:

```
      ← p(X), q(a).
      ← q(X), q(a).
      ← q(a).
```

At this point, the goal fails and we backtrack to the previous goal. Because q(a) failed, it is selected again, and fails immediately. Normally, q(X) would have been retried, leading to useless extra computation. We then backtrack to the first goal, where q(a) is selected (and fails) once more. A total of eight unifications are attempted, instead of thirteen, for the conventional algorithm (the saving can be made arbitrarily large by adding more clauses to procedure p). If this example was part of a larger computation, which previously bound the argument of 'q' to 'a', then we would quickly backtrack to that point. Alternatively, q(a) may have been an introduced atom when some other atom, say p(a), was selected. In this case, q(a) would be selected until we backtrack to the goal containing p(a). P(a) would then be selected again and would fail, thus continuing the process.

This rule can also interact favourably with other computation rules, in a way in which other intelligent backtracking cannot. We shall use our eight queens example again. Suppose we have sufficient control information to delay the test (*safe*) when it is insufficiently instantiated, but it is called after the generator (*perm*). When the program is run, a complete permutation is generated with the first two queen positions in conflicting positions. *Safe* is then called and quickly fails. With conventional systems, many more permutations would be generated before the second queen position is changed, taking time exponential in the number of queens. An intelligent backtracking system would analyse the failure and immediately backtrack to the point where the second queen position was chosen, taking linear time. However, another complete permutation would be generated before *safe* is called again.

With our proposal, *safe* would be called after each backtrack of the generator. After a few calls it fails, forcing further backtracking. This is slower than intelligent backtracking, though the time taken is still linear in the number of queens. When the call that decided the position of the second queen is finally backtracked over, *safe* is called again, but does not fail. Instead, it delays. The generator is then restarted, but whenever a new queen position is decided, the test can be woken, resulting in a more efficient algorithm. Thus our variant of the killer heuristic not only often performs within a constant factor of intelligent backtracking, but also has the ability to detect calls which tend to fail on the fly, and initiate coroutining with them. Such a rule should therefore be implemented in conjunction with other computation rules which complement each other.

One criticism of intelligent backtracking is that it only reacts intelligently to mistakes when they are finally discovered, rather than avoiding them in the first place, as sophisticated computation rules try to do. The scheme we propose attempts to avoid mistakes and also behaves sensibly, by backtracking quickly, when this fails. It can also effectively learn from its mistakes, by reordering calls to tests and generators. Furthermore, the intelligent backtracking component is included in the computation rule, and requires very little additional overhead.

4.5. Summary

We have developed a more general model of the execution of PROLOG systems with extra control facilities, and shown the previous theoretical results still hold. This corrects the previous over-simplification, and allows us to see possible new extensions to the system more easily. We have give an example that shows how a relatively simple computation rule can do far more than was previously thought possible.

5. AN OVERVIEW OF PROLOG CONTROL RULES

5.1. Introduction

Since Kowalski's seminal paper, "Algorithm = Logic + Control" [Kowalski 79], there have been several implementations of PROLOG with more control facilities than the conventional systems. This trend seems to be continuing. In the past, the design of these systems has been justified by examples of how programmers can implement efficient algorithms using simple logic. We have gone a step further and shown how control can often be generated automatically. In this chapter, we take a much broader view. We examine many control primitives and heuristics, to identify their strengths and weaknesses. We use the term *control rule* for these individual components of complete computation rules. Our attention is restricted to control rules for HSLD resolution. We hope the discussion and conclusions here will contribute to the design of logic programming systems with better control components in the future. It may also give some ideas to those attempting a more theoretical treatment of control and efficiency. We make one contribution to the theory, but much more work is needed. Unfortunately, it seems to be a very difficult area.

The main part of this chapter introduces some general properties that we should like computation rules to exhibit. The extent to which each control rule contributes to these properties is discussed, and used for a simple classification. Finally, an idealized combination of control rules is suggested, and some likely modifications, for an actual implementation, are mentioned. First, however, we give some programming examples which will be referred to in the discussion.

5.2. Program Examples

The following selection of programming examples, from the literature, illustrates the kinds of problems that can be solved efficiently by using a flexible control strategy.

```
perm([ ], [ ]).
perm(X.Y, U.V) :- perm(Z, V), delete(U, X.Y, Z).

delete(A, A.L, L).
delete(X, A.B.L, A.R) :- delete(X, B.L, R).
```

These procedures define the permutation relation on lists that we used earlier. In fact, there are several similar definitions. One reason for this is that the relation is symmetric, so the arguments of *perm* may be swapped without affecting the least fixed point semantics. We would therefore like the control we use to ensure that either order works in practice. [Elcock 83] shows how difficult it is to write a multi-use definition of *perm* using the conventional PROLOG computation rule. If *perm* is called with the second argument a variable, the execution of *delete* should proceed ahead of *perm* but if the first argument is a variable, *perm* should proceed ahead of *delete*. The word variable here can be replaced by "list with a variable tail". Partially instantiated data structures, such as this, tend to make control more difficult.

queen(X) :– perm(1.2.3.4.5.6.7.8.[ ], X), safe(X).

safe([ ]).
safe(N.L) :– safe(L), nodiag(N, 1, L).

nodiag(_, _, [ ]).
nodiag(B, D, N.L) :–
        D =\= N–B, D =\= B–N,
        D1 is D + 1, nodiag(B, D1, L).

Using *perm*, we can write a program to solve the eight queens problem. The desirable form of control discussed most in the literature, and which we illustrated earlier, is for *perm* and *delete* to generate the list of queen positions one at a time, and for *safe* and *nodiag* to test if the new queen position is unsafe. If the arguments in the initial call to *perm* are swapped, a more efficient strategy is possible: delay calls to *delete* and =\= until the end, then do the calls to *delete*, resuming the instantiated calls to =\= at each stage.

    sameleaves(T1, T2) :– leaves(T1, L), leaves(T2, L).

leaves(leaf(X), [X]).
leaves(t(leaf(X), T), X.L) :– leaves(T, L).
leaves(t(t(LL,LR),R), L) :– leaves(t(LL,t(LR,R)), L).

This program can be used to check whether two trees have the same list of leaf tags. The desired form of control is for the two calls to *leaves* to coroutine. Whenever one further instantiates the list of leaf tags, the other should check if the newly added tag is the next tag in the other tree. Either call can be the generator at each stage. This program can easily be extended to any number of trees.

    grandparent(G, C) :– parent(G, P), parent(P, C).

ancestor(P, C) :– parent(P, C).
ancestor(A, D) :– parent(P, D), ancestor(A, P).

Here we define the *grandparent* and *ancestor* procedures using *parent*, which we assume is defined with a collection of facts. *Grandparent* can be used to find the grandparents or grandchildren of a given person. For efficiency, it is much better to make the second call to *parent* first when *grandparent* is used to find the grandparents of someone. For finding grandchildren, however, the textual order is best.

Ancestor poses some rather difficult optimization problems. For finding the ancestors of someone, *parent* should always be called first. Calling *ancestor* first causes an infinite loop. In fact, infinite loops can occur even when *parent* is called first if, according to the program, someone is their own ancestor. The program can also be used for finding descendants, though there are even more difficulties. If parent is called first it is very inefficient but no infinite loop results (provided no-one is their own ancestor). Calling *ancestor* first is efficient but eventually results in an infinite loop.

The best form of control for finding descendants is for *ancestor* to be called first initially then for it to be called last. The point where the control changes should be the maximum number of generations between the person and their descendants. This is not usually known beforehand. The order in which the several calls to *parent* are done should be the reverse of the order in which they were introduced. If the following (equivalent) recursive clause for *ancestor* is used, finding descendants is easier but finding ancestors is more difficult.

ancestor(A, D) :– parent(A, C), ancestor(C, D).

5.3. Desirable Properties of Computation Rules

5.3.1. Minimizing the Search Tree Size

The one obvious overriding property that we wish computation rules to exhibit, is to make the search tree of the refutation procedure as small as possible. Unfortunately, except in very simple cases, this is not amenable to implementation. Usually, we cannot even find heuristics directly related to the size of the tree. It is therefore desirable to have some slightly lower level rules. In the next two sub-sections we introduce heuristics which are reasonably general, but are useful for the design and classification of implementable control rules.

5.3.2. Detecting Failure

For goals that can finitely fail, computation rules should select atoms that lead to failure quickly. Solving other atoms merely delays the inevitable failure. Several heuristics and language constructs have been devised to help select failing subgoals quickly. We have already mentioned the theoretical work done on making HSLD resolution complete with respect to finite failure.

5.3.3. Avoiding Failure

There is a slightly more subtle rule which applies more to goals which have solutions. The number and length of successful derivations of a goal does not depend on the computation rule (see [Lloyd 84b]), which tends to suggest that the computation rule is unimportant for successful goals. However, although the success branches of the tree are fixed, the number and length of other branches is not. The rule, therefore, is to avoid creation of unnecessary failure (and infinite) branches, as much as possible. We believe the explicit statement of this rule provides new insights into the control problem of logic programming.

5.4. Control Rules

We now discuss a large selection of control rules mentioned in the literature. They are put into three groups, under the same headings as the previous section. As we shall point out, a few primitives have different aspects which affect avoiding and detecting failure. These are discussed in the sub-section they most contribute to. There is another way in which our classification can be obscured too. If a control rule tends to select (or avoid selecting) one type of subgoal, then the selection of all other types is affected. Such side-effects should be ignored.

5.4.1. Minimizing the Search Tree Size

In this section we mention two extreme cases of detecting and avoiding failure which are optimal. Heuristics for optimizing relational database queries are also discussed. With more special case analysis, this section could probably be expanded in the future. A closely related area is that of constraint systems and equation solving. Methods for solving conjunctions of equations and constraints are well known, though they do not quite fit into the framework of HSLD resolution and computation rules.

5.4.1.1. Select Calls Which Fail

Sub-goals which match with no clauses should clearly be selected immediately. This rule was implemented in METALOG [Dincbas 80], which continually tested whether any atoms had no matching clauses. No method has yet been found for implementing this rule without significant overheads. The feature does not appear in a description of a more efficient implementation of METALOG [Dincbas 84]. In systems which avoid failure better, the benefits are also reduced.

5.4.1.2. Select Locally Deterministic Calls

As before, *locally deterministic* means the calls match with one clause, even if the subsequent computation may contain choice points. Selecting locally deterministic calls is optimal for goals with some solution(s), since no extra failure branches are created. This is one of the few theoretical results concerning the size of (H)SLD trees and we outline a proof below.

Lemma (Determinism switching) If S is an SLD tree for $P \cup \{G\}$, D is a locally deterministic subgoal of G, and D is selected at level two of S, then there exists an SLD tree, T, for $P \cup \{G\}$, which has no more nodes than S and has D selected at level one (the root).

Proof For simplicity, we ignore the order of subgoals, and assume D is selected in the leftmost branch. In the diagram below, the goals are written with the selected subgoal first.

$$
\begin{array}{cc}
S & T \\[4pt]
\leftarrow C,D,.. & \leftarrow D,C,.. \\
\diagup \quad | \ldots \diagdown & | \\
\leftarrow D,.. \quad S_2 \ldots S_n & \leftarrow C,.. \\
| & \diagup \ | \ldots \diagdown \\
S_1 & T_1 \quad T_2 \ldots T_n
\end{array}
$$

We construct the sub-trees, T_i, by selecting the same atoms as in S_i, where possible. T_1 is the same as S_1, since the root goals are the same (up to renaming). For other sub-trees, initially (at the root), the parent of the node in S is in the form $\leftarrow C_1,...,C_j,D$, say, and the parent node in T is $\leftarrow (C_1,...,C_j,D_1,...,D_k)\theta$, where $D_1,...,D_k$ is the body of the rule that D matches, and θ is the substitution applied at that call.

Because of the extra substitution, the head of the rule which was applied in S, may not unify with the selected subgoal in T. In this case, T has an empty sub-tree corresponding to a non-empty sub-tree in S.

If the unification succeeds, there are two possible cases. Firstly, if the selected subgoal in the parent is D, then the goal in the node of S is ← $(C_1,...,C_j,D_1,...,D_k)\theta$, the same as the parent node in T. Thus, the sub-tree T can be made one node smaller than the sub-tree in S (an example of this is T_1 and S_1 plus its parent).

The second case occurs when one of the Cs is selected in S. We then just select the same subgoal in T. For each child, we are in a similar situation to before. There is just a different set of Cs and a different substitution, so we can continue constructing T in the same way. With this construction, T can have no more nodes than S. □

Theorem If the root goal of an SLD tree, S, has a locally deterministic subgoal, D, which is selected somewhere in the tree, then there is a tree with D selected at the root which is as small as S.

Proof Apply the determinism switching lemma repeatedly. □

Corollary If G has at least one solution and has a deterministic subgoal, D, then selecting D first is optimal.

Proof Since G has a solution, every SLD tree has a success branch and must select D somewhere. Therefore, by the theorem, there is a tree as small as any other, with D selected at the root. □

These results are also true of HSLD resolution, though we will not give complete proofs here. What is needed is a lemma that shows that if D is selected with several other calls, then it is as efficient to select D alone. The proof is very like that of the determinism switching lemma.

One problem with implementation is efficiently finding out which calls are deterministic. We showed previously how automatically generated control information can force many procedures to be deterministic for all calls. We discuss this further in the section on wait declarations. By slightly extending the analysis, some deterministic calls to other procedures can also be detected. Most of these are actually amenable to partial evaluation, which is even better.

5.4.1.3. Minimizing the Number of Matching Clauses

Given that calls with zero and one matching clauses should be selected, it seems obvious to consider greater numbers of clauses. One heuristic is to select calls with the lowest number of matching clauses first (assuming this can be determined efficiently). This is the basis for the query optimization of [Warren 81] (see the section on database queries). For recursive procedures, the rule is much less effective. It is very common for there to be several calls matching two clauses, only some of which create extra failure branches. The following goal is typical of those encountered with the eight queens program. Although all calls match with two clauses, calling *safe*, *nodiag* or *perm* would create failure branches, whereas *delete* would not.

← safe(L), nodiag(N, 1, L), perm(Z, L), delete(N, [1,2,3,4,5,6,7,8], Z).

This heuristic is not particularly effective with recursive procedures and, for database queries, better methods also exist.

5.4.1.4. Database Queries

Given a goal consisting of calls to database procedures, we showed how formulas for the number of calls and unifications needed to find all solutions can be derived. They are heuristics, based on some assumptions about probabilities of various matches being independent, etc. The formulas can be minimized to find the best computation rule. Calls to large database procedures should generally be delayed until less expensive calls have been done. The optimal computation rule can then be applied. This allows the maximum flexibility and calls to procedures with rules can be coroutined where it is desirable.

Other systems have used an approximation to the formula for minimizing the number of calls in less flexible ways. This was first done for query optimization in CHAT-80 [Warren 81] where the subgoals in the top level query are reordered. If all top level calls are to database procedures, the result is usually optimal but calls to procedures with rules may cause inefficiency. [Stabler 83] extended this idea to reordering rules in the program. It reduces the possible inefficiency of the CHAT-80 approach but is not optimal since coroutining is not possible. Also, procedures that are used in several ways are not easily catered for. The reduced number of unifications and disc accesses from our method should easily outweigh its greater overheads.

5.4.2. Detecting Failure

5.4.2.1. Call Tests as Soon as Possible

Tests fail more often than other calls so, to detect failure quickly, they should be called as soon as possible. For example, our preprocessor uses some heuristics to detect tests and re-orders subgoals to ensure that they are called quickly. One problem, of course, is that the tests should not be called before they are sufficiently instantiated. To this extent, calling tests quickly conflicts with avoiding failure.

5.4.2.2. Resume Woken Calls as Soon as Possible

This is related to the usual implementation of the rule for calling tests quickly. Often, an attempt to call a test is made before it is sufficiently instantiated. The call is delayed and the variables that need to be instantiated are marked. When they are bound, we say the test is woken. It should then be called quickly. If the woken call is not a test, however, this is not necessarily a good idea. In systems where tests are recognized, it may be worth giving priority to woken tests.

5.4.2.3. Eager Consumers

IC-PROLOG's *eager consumer* annotations [Clark 79] can be used to implement the ideas of the previous two sections. They also contribute to avoiding failure, by delaying insufficiently instantiated tests. The effect of placing an eager consumer annotation on some variable of a subgoal is, in effect, to increase the priority of the computation of that subgoal. The subgoal is called initially and if it is ever delayed, it is resumed at the earliest possible moment.

The whole computation of the subgoal is delayed if an attempt is made to further instantiate the annotated variable. This has the unfortunate consequence of delaying instantiated tests in cases where the annotated subgoal calls several tests. For example, if *safe* is made an eager consumer in the eight queens program, only one call to *nodiag* is made when a new queen is added. This can be avoided to some extent by using other control primitives to compensate (pseudo-parallelism, for example). A similar problem is caused by the restriction that only one subgoal can be a designated consumer of a particular variable. For the same leaves program, this is sufficient, but if the program is extended to check three or more trees, not all the computations can be coroutined.

Delaying part of the computation when it is about to instantiate an annotated variable is justified from the point of view of avoiding failure. However, the extent of delaying (the whole subgoal computation) and the single consumer restriction adversely affect failure detection. One advantage of eager consumers is the "inheritance" of the annotation to sub-terms. This means procedures can behave differently, depending on the call, and fewer annotations are needed.

5.4.2.4. The Killer Heuristic

Our variant of the killer heuristic, used as an example of a computation rule for HSLD resolution, is specifically targeted at detecting failure. When a failure is found at one point in the search tree, this is used to find failure more quickly in other parts of the tree. Our previous example showed how it can act like a simple form of intelligent backtracking, and also lead to tests being called before generators.

5.4.2.5. Fairness

[Lassez 84] shows that SLD resolution is complete with respect to finite failure, assuming a fairness condition. We extended this result to HSLD resolution. Depth first rules and rules for most primitives that delay calls are unfair. There are two aspects of fairness which could affect practical systems. The first concerns avoiding infinite loops by failing where possible. The theory does not say how quickly the failure is found, but when no better heuristics are applicable, a fair computation rule will ensure that the failure will be found eventually.

The second aspect concerns completeness. Several control primitives can delay calls indefinitely, so even if a goal has solutions or can finitely fail, the computation may terminate without doing all calls. With a fair computation rule, this would not be possible. The completeness we obtain is obviously beneficial. However, for debugging purposes, especially for finding possible infinite loops, it would be helpful if an option were available to store some information, or trace the calls which would not otherwise have been done.

5.4.2.6. Breadth First

The simplest way to ensure fairness is to use a *breadth first* computation rule. This is the main idea of *sidetracking*, described in [Pereira 79]. It can be implemented by having a queue of subgoals, rather than a stack. Usually, generators and tests produce and consume (respectively) data structures at similar rates, like *safe* and *perm* in the eight queens problem. Typically, one level of recursion corresponds to one level of functor nesting. This implies that a breadth first rule would have a fairly small delay between generating and testing, so failures are found relatively quickly. Another example of this is the same leaves program with two or more trees. The worst case is for the leaves of one tree to be produced twice as fast as the others and the average case is much better.

Unfortunately, a strict breadth first rule is very poor at avoiding failure, especially when tests are called before generators. Typically, a breadth first rule results in SLD trees with many failure branches but no infinite branches. This contrasts with depth first rules, for which the tree size depends very much of the order of subgoals in the program. The best order can result in very small trees but other orders often result in infinite trees. With modifications to avoid failure, we believe a breadth first rule can make significant improvements to failure detection, and can ensure fairness.

5.4.2.7. Pseudo Parallelism

IC-PROLOG's // connective has a declarative reading of "and", but the two (or more) subgoals it connects are computed in pseudo-parallel. The computation rule alternates between selecting atoms from each of the different sub-computations. The same control has also been used as an example of the power of the meta-interpreter approach to control used by EPILOG [Porto 82] and Two-Level PROLOG [Porto 84].

Pseudo-parallelism ensures a form of fairness at the top level of the computation, but the sub-computations may use unfair rules. If // is used for all and-connectives, the result is a fair computation rule. However, if one sub-computation is a generator and the other contains several tests, the execution of the tests tends to lag behind the generator. For example, when the generator completes in the eight queens program, only 14 to 42 percent of the tests have been called (depending on the solution to the generator). For some programs, pseudo-parallelism can perform very well but, in general, we consider breadth first is a better choice.

5.4.2.8. Avoid Left Recursion

We suggested this rule for MU-PROLOG earlier and it is also advisable in PROLOG M, as we mentioned. Because most PROLOG systems uses a depth first control rule, left recursion tends to result in infinite loops. By placing recursive calls last, failures are detected instead. Actually, left recursion is desirable in some situations, such as *perm* in our alternative eight queens example. The problem is that left recursion is a pathological case for failure detection with a depth first rule. The solution is to improve failure detection in general, not ban left recursion. With a breadth first control rule, left recursion is not a problem, since the non-recursive calls are done just after the recursive call.

5.4.3. Avoiding Failure

5.4.3.1. Freeze

The main reason for delaying subgoals in PROLOG is to avoid creating failure branches, and there are very many primitives which enable this. The simplest is *freeze* of PROLOG II [Colmerauer 82]. The ! annotation of IC-PROLOG and *constrain* primitive of LM-PROLOG [Carlsson 83] are very similar, and *freeze* can also be implemented simply using primitives available in other systems. It can be implemented with wait declarations as follows.

```
?- wait freeze(0, 1).
freeze(xxxx, _) :- fail.
freeze(X, C) :- call(C).
```

Freeze is used to delay a subgoal until a particular variable is bound to a non-variable. Because it only delays a single call, the eight queens can be made more efficient than with eager consumers, though *freeze* is needed for four different subgoals.

However, because the control is not inherited to sub-terms of the variable, the same leaves program cannot easily be made efficient. Two versions of *leaves* are needed: one the same as before, and the other with a call to *freeze*, so it delays when the leaf list is uninstantiated. If the original version is called last, one or more of the delaying versions can coroutine with it efficiently. Also, because *freeze* only waits for one variable (like many other primitives), it is less useful for multi-use procedures and cannot make *perm* work in both ways.

5.4.3.2. Lazy Producers

IC-PROLOG's *lazy producers* provide a powerful method of avoiding failure and, to a lesser extent, detecting failure. A lazy producer annotation on a variable in a subgoal gives the computation of the subgoal a lower priority, and prevents all other calls from binding the variable. Like eager consumers, the effect is inherited. When another call attempts to construct the annotated variable, that call is delayed. The producer is then executed until it binds the variable, then the previously delayed call is resumed.

The choice of which call is resumed does not help avoid failure: if anything, it is a bad choice. If the call is a test, however, the choice helps detect failure. For this reason, lazy producers can often be used in the same way as eager consumers. This overlapping of control rules can cause confusion, we believe. It also means that coroutining between a generator and multiple tests is still difficult to implement.

5.4.3.3. Wait Declarations

Under this heading, we include the wait declarations of MU-PROLOG and also the algorithm used for generating them automatically, described previously. We believe it is a major contribution to avoiding failure. The effect of wait declarations is local, like *freeze*, but they can be used to delay a call until one of several argument sets is sufficiently instantiated. This added flexibility makes it possible for procedures such as *perm* to work in multiple ways without creating unnecessary failure branches. The heuristic for generating wait declarations also produces the best form of control in the goal from the eight queens program we gave earlier. The failure producing subgoals (*safe, nodiag* and *perm*) are delayed by automatically generated wait declarations whereas *delete* is not.

Automatically generated wait declarations also interact very favourably with the rule for selecting deterministic calls first. Wait declarations cause many calls to delay until they are deterministic and these calls can easily be detected by a preprocessor. With the eight queens program, calls to all procedures except *delete* are forced to be deterministic. Using this information with our alternative eight queens program, failure branches from *safe, nodiag* and *perm* are eliminated and those from *delete* are delayed until the end. This is optimal up to the order of calls to *delete* and =\=.

However, there are situations where generated wait declarations delay calls unnecessarily or where wait declaration cannot be generated at all (such as in *ancestor*). The first case causes incompleteness, which can be overcome by fairness. Rather than wait declarations delaying calls indefinitely, they could just greatly decrease the call's priority. This can have an arbitrarily small effect on efficiency while retaining completeness and termination where possible. The second case occurs where there is a potential infinite loop that cannot be stopped by wait declarations. Fairness can also avoid many such loops and the priority should usually be reduced greatly too, for avoiding failure. With this control, *parent* would always be called before *ancestor*.

5.4.3.4. Triggers and When Declarations

Triggers were suggested in [Warren 79] but never pursued. They are similar to wait declaration in that they can delay a call until one of several subsets of arguments are non-variables. The distinction between "non-variable" and "sufficiently instantiated" (which depends on the clause heads) means than wait declarations can be used and automatically generated in more situations. An advantage of triggers is that they can can be compiled more easily. When declarations also depend of whether various parts of the call are variables or not, but they can contain more structure than triggers. They can be compiled, though not as easily as triggers, and have even more flexibility than wait declarations.

5.4.3.5. Reordering Clause Bodies

The idea here is to use different orders of the subgoals in clause bodies depending on the way the procedure is called. The main application is for avoiding failure in multi-use procedures, though the static reordering of subgoals in the MU-PROLOG preprocessor, for detecting failure, is very similar. [Shoham 84] uses the idea for "inverting" procedures that should be multi-use.

The "linking control with use" annotations of IC-PROLOG allow the programmer to write several different versions of a clause, and specify which one should be used for each type of call. In the *grandparent* procedure, for example, the two different orders for calling *parent* can be implemented. If used in all possible places, the program can be made considerably larger. An alternative is for the different orders to be determined automatically, by some form of data flow analysis, and possibly augmented by our wait declaration algorithm.

Reordering clause bodies is very useful for multi-use procedures, though partially instantiated data structures can cause inefficiency. However, coroutining is not possible, because no global reordering of the entire goal is done. Thus reordering clauses is not sufficient for optimal database query processing or detecting failure quickly in cases such as the eight queens and same leaves programs. The addition of our rule for database procedures or wait declarations results in a very non-orthogonal system. Clause reordering plus eager consumers seems a reasonable choice, though it is not ideal.

5.4.3.6. Delaying System Predicates

In MU-PROLOG, partially instantiated calls to system predicates such as < always delay. In IC-PROLOG, they act as generators instead, often creating extra failure branches. By waiting for the variables to be instantiated by other calls, failure branches can be avoided and control like that in our alternative eight queens example (with =\= delaying) can be used. In MU-PROLOG, if the variables are not bound by other calls, the system tests are never woken, so completeness is lost for some types of goals. It would be preferable for the system tests to be called eventually, if possible.

5.5. Discussion

With most systems, the methods available for avoiding failure are not flexible enough. To delay the calls that create failure branches, other calls must be delayed also. This is manifest is two ways. Firstly, in the delaying of whole sub-computations in IC-PROLOG. Secondly, most primitives only allow subgoals to wait for a single variable to be bound, even though many procedures can work efficiently consuming several different subsets of their arguments. Wait declarations are an exception. They only delay single calls, and are flexible enough to enable multi-use procedures. Partly because of this, they can also be generated automatically. The deficiencies in the algorithm can be partially compensated for by having a fair computation rule, so calls delayed by wait declarations are still done eventually.

There are also deficiencies with failure detection, despite this being well understood. Because of delaying whole sub-computations and the single eager consumer limitation in IC-PROLOG, failure detection is impaired when multiple tests are needed. With other systems especially, multiple (potential) generators, such as the same leaves program, are not handled well. Left recursion also causes problems. Both these areas can be improved by using a breadth first rule. This performs slightly worse than a more controlled coroutine approach, but requires no programmer intervention.

Our idealized system has three major features. Firstly, calls that are likely to create extra failure branches are delayed. Secondly, other calls that are likely to fail are called first. Thirdly, the computation rule is fair, so even calls likely to create failure branches are called eventually. We propose a hierarchy of calls as follows:

(1)   Calls which have previously lead to finding failure (the killer heuristic)

(2)   Woken calls

(3)   Tests

(4)   Other deterministic calls

(5)   Nondeterministic calls

(6)   Calls to database procedures

(7)   Calls to procedures for which wait declarations cannot be generated

(8)   Calls delayed by wait declarations

(9)   Delayed calls to system predicates

The optimal order in which to call the database procedures can be determined, and other types of calls should be done in a breadth first manner, for failure finding and fairness. Furthermore, a lower priority call should be done after some number of calls (say 1000) of the next higher priority, to ensure fairness. For implementation reasons, several of these categories may be coalesced. The most obvious two are tests and other deterministic calls. Also, it may be decided that the advantages of the killer heuristic do not outweigh the costs of implementing it (with HSLD resolution, slightly more information needs to be kept for delayed calls). Replacing wait declarations by when declarations, or some similar primitive, is also possible.

Another practical consideration concerns various system programming tasks, that are normally implemented in PROLOG. With breadth first control, it is not possible to write utilities such as *consult*, the user interface, and *not*, because they rely on non-logical system procedures like *assert*, *read*, *write* and *cut*, for which the order of calls is critical. Intelligent backtracking often has similar effects. The solution we propose for this is two have two types of procedures, distinguished by some type of declaration. With one type, the full flexibility of the control could be used. With the other, the execution of the subgoals must be strictly left to right. Within the computation of a subgoal coroutining could take place but the subgoal, must be solved entirely before the next one is called. If this is not possible a control error should occur. Similarly, intelligent backtracking should be localized to each subgoal.

5.6. Conclusions

Current PROLOG systems with extra control facilities have been designed in a ad hoc manner, relying mostly on a few example programs. We have introduced some more general principles on which control rules can be judged. This shows the weaknesses and strengths of current control rules much more clearly, and should be of useful in the design of future systems which further exploit the advantages of flexible control strategies.

REFERENCES

[Apt 82]

K. R. Apt and M. H. Van Emden, "Contributions to the Theory of Logic Programming", *Journal of the ACM 29*, 3 (July 1982), 841-862. Also available as a Technical Report CS-80-13 from the University of Waterloo, Canada.

[Babb 83]

E. Babb, "Finite Computation Principal – An Alternative Method of Adapting Resolution for Logic Programming", *Proceedings of Workshop on Logic Programming*, Algarve, Portugal, 1983.

[Balbin 86]

I. Balbin and K. Ramamohanarao, "A Differential Approach to Query Optimisation in Recursive Deductive Databases", Technical Report 86/7, Department of Computer Science, University of Melbourne, 1986.

[Bellia 83]

M. Bellia, G. Levi and M. Martelli, "On Compiling Prolog Programs on Demand-Driven Architectures", *Proceedings of the 2nd Workshop on Logic Programming*, Algarve, Portugal, 1983, 518-535.

[Bowen 82]

D. L. Bowen, L. Byrd, F. C. N. Pereira, L. M. Pereira and D. H. D. Warren, "Decsystem-10 Prolog User's Manual", Occasional Paper 27, Department of Artificial Intelligence, University of Edinburgh, Scotland, November, 1982.

[Brough 84]

D. R. Brough and A. Walker, "Some Practical Properties of Logic Programming Interpreters", *Proceedings of the 1984 Conference on Fifth Generation Computer Systems*, Tokyo, Japan, November, 1984.

[Bruynooghe 83]

M. Bruynooghe and L. M. Pereira, "Deductive Revision by Intelligent Backtracking", UNL-10/83, Universidade Nova Lisboa, Lisbon, Portugal, 1983. Also in "Issues in Prolog Implementation", J. Campbell (ed.).

[Carlsson 83]

M. Carlsson and K. M. Kahn, "LM-Prolog User Manual", UPMAIL Technical Report 24, Computer Science Department, Uppsala University, 1983.

[Clark 78]

K. L. Clark, "Negation as Failure", in *Logic and Databases*, H. Gallaire and J. Minker (editor), Plenum Press, 1978.

[Clark 79]

K. L. Clark and F. G. McCabe, "The Control Facilities of IC-Prolog", in *Expert Systems in the Microelectronic Age*, D. Michie (editor), University of Edinburgh, Scotland, 1979, 153-167.

6. CONCLUSION

Our most significant contribution to the control problem is the algorithm for generating wait declarations for recursive procedures. The main property of interest is its effectiveness at avoiding failure. It forces many procedures to be deterministic, and others are prevented from constructing certain arguments. A side effect of this, is that the algorithm can also be used as a basis for recognising tests. Subgoals may then be reordered, so as to enhance failure detection. We have combined these two factors in a very effective preprocessor for MU-PROLOG. It has proved useful for providing control in several programming styles.

Our algorithm has also provided a target for the more theoretical approach of capture rules. Heuristic methods will be at the forefront of control for some time, but they can be understood better, and hopefully improved on, by the theoretical work. However, it may be a mistake to concentrate only on proving termination, and ignoring efficiency. Fairness is a simpler way to deal with nontermination alone. We need to greatly increase our theoretical understanding of efficiency in (H)SLD resolution though, unfortunately, it is a very difficult area. Our only result concerns locally deterministic calls. Even with simplifying assumptions, optimizing a database goal is a hard problem.

This makes approaches such as ours in Chapter 5 more important. Until we have a better theoretical understanding, we need heuristics in order to build better systems. They may also be a starting point for theoretical work. For example, it may be possible to find classes of programs for which some computation rule detects or avoids failure optimally. Finally, we feel that HSLD resolution warrants further investigation. It offers a much richer set of computation rules, with a modest additional overhead.

[Clark 80]

K. L. Clark and F. G. McCabe, "IC-Prolog – Language Features", in *Workshop on Logic Programming*, S. Tarnlund (editor), Debrecen, Hungary, July 1980. Also in Logic Programming, Clark and Tarnlund (eds.), Academic Press, 1982.

[Clark 83a]

K. L. Clark and S. Gregory, "PARLOG: A Parallel Logic Programming Language", Technical Report TR-83-5, Imperial College, London, 1983.

[Clark 83b]

K. L. Clark, "Predicate Logic as a Computational Formalism", Research Report, DOC, Imperial College, London, 1983.

[Clocksin 84]

W. F. Clocksin and C. S. Mellish, *Programming in Prolog*, Springer Verlag (2nd Edition), New York, 1984.

[Colmerauer 82]

A. Colmerauer, "Prolog-II Manuel de Reference et Modele Theorique", Groupe Intelligence Artificelle, Univerisite d'Aix-Marseille II, 1982.

[Dahl 80]

V. Dahl, "Two Solutions for the Negation Problem", in *Workshop on Logic Programming*, S. A. Tarnlund (editor), Debrecen, Hungary, July 1980.

[Dahl 82]

V. Dahl, "On Database Systems Development Through Logic", *ACM Transactions on Database Systems 7*, 1 (March 1982), 102-123.

[de Rougemont 84]

M. de Rougemont, "From Logic to Logic Programming", *Proceedings of AIMSA-84*, Varna, Bulgaria, September, 1984.

[Dincbas 80]

M. Dincbas, "The METALOG Problem-Solving System: An Informal Presentation", in *Workshop on Logic Programming*, S. A. Tarnlund (editor), Debrecen, Hungary, July 1980, 80-91.

[Dincbas 84]

M. Dincbas and J. P. Le Pape, "Metacontrol of Logic Programs in METALOG", *International Conference On Fifth Generation Computer Systems*, November 1984.

[Elcock 83]

E. W. Elcock, "The Pragmatics of Prolog: Some Comments", *Proceedings of Workshop on Logic Programming*, Algarve, Portugal, 1983.

[Foster 69]

A. Foster and E. W. Elcock, "Absys1: An Incremental Compiler for Assertions: An Introduction", in *Machine Intelligence 4*, B. Meltzer and D. Mitchie (editor), Edinburgh University Press, 1969.

[Gallaire 80]

    H. Gallaire and C. Lasserre, "A Control Metalanguage for Logic Programming", *Workshop on Logic Programming*, Debrecen, Hungary, 1980, 123-132. Also in Logic Programming, Clark and Tarnlund (eds.), Academic Press, 1982.

[Gallaire 83]

    H. Gallaire, "Logic Databases versus Deductive Databases", *Proceedings of Workshop on Logic Programming*, Algarve, Portugal, 1983.

[Gregory 80]

    S. Gregory, "Towards the Compilation of Annotated Logic Programs", Report CCD 80/16, Imperial College, London, 1980.

[Hill 74]

    R. Hill, "LUSH-Resolution and Its Completeness", DCS Memo, No. 78, Department of Artificial Intelligence, University of Edinburgh, 1974.

[Jaffar 83]

    J. Jaffar, J. L. Lassez and J. W. Lloyd, "Completeness of the Negation As Failure Rule", *Proceedings of the International Joint Conference on Artificial Intelligence*, Karlsruhe, Germany, 1983, 500-506. Also available as Technical Report 83/1, Department of Computer Science, University of Melbourne, Australia.

[Kahn 84]

    K. M. Kahn, "A Primitive for the Control of Logic Programs", *Proceedings of the International IEEE Conference on Logic Programming*, Atlantic City, 1984.

[Khabaza 84]

    T. Khabaza, "Negation as Failure and Parallellism", *Proceedings of the International IEEE Conference on Logic Programming*, Atlantic City, 1984.

[Kowalski 79]

    R. A. Kowalski, "Algorithm = Logic + Control", *Communications of the ACM 22*, 7 (July 1979), 424-436.

[Lassez 84]

    J. L. Lassez and M. J. Maher, "Closures and Fairness in the Semantics of Programming Logic", *Theoretical Computer Science 29* (1984), 167-184. Also as Technical Report 83/3, Department of Computer Science, University of Melbourne.

[Lloyd 83]

    J. W. Lloyd, "An Introduction To Deductive Data Base Systems", *Australian Computer Journal 15*, 2 (1983). Also a Technical Report, Department of Computer Science, University of Melbourne, 1982.

[Lloyd 84a]

    J. W. Lloyd and R. W. Topor, "Making Prolog More Expressive", *Journal of Logic Programming 3* (1984). Also Technical Report 84/8, Department Of Computer Science, University Of Melbourne.

[Lloyd 84b]

J. W. Lloyd, *Foundations Of Logic Programming*, Springer Verlag, 1984.

[Mellish 81]

C. S. Mellish, "Automatic Generation of Mode Declarations in Prolog Programs", *Workshop on Logic Programming*, Long Beach, Los Angeles, September 1981.

[MIP 86]

J.A. Thom and J.A. Zobel (Eds.), "NU-Prolog 1.0 Reference Manual", Technical Report 86/10, Machine Intelligence Project, Department of Computer Science, University of Melbourne, 1986.

[Naish 82]

L. Naish, "An Introduction to MU-PROLOG", Technical Report 82/2, Department of Computer Science, University of Melbourne, 1982. Revised in 1983.

[Naish 83a]

L. Naish, "Automatic Generation of Control for Logic Programs", Technical Report 83/6, Department of Computer Science, University of Melbourne, 1983.

[Naish 83b]

L. Naish and J. A. Thom, "The MU-PROLOG Deductive Database", Technical Report 83/10, Department of Computer Science, University of Melbourne, 1983.

[Naish 84a]

L. Naish, "Heterogeneous SLD Resolution", *Journal of Logic Programming 1*, 4 (1984). Also Technical Report 84/1, Department of Computer Science, University of Melbourne.

[Naish 84b]

L. Naish and J. L. Lassez, "Most Specific Logic Programs", Technical Report 84/9, Department of Computer Science, University of Melbourne, in preparation.

[Naish 84c]

L. Naish, "PROLOG Control Rules", Technical Report 84/13, Department of Computer Science, University of Melbourne, 1984.

[Naish 85a]

L. Naish, "MU-PROLOG 3.2db Reference Manual", Technical Report, Department of Computer Science, University of Melbourne, 1985.

[Naish 85b]

L. Naish, "Automating Control for Logic Programs", *The Journal of Logic Programming 2*, 3 (1985).

[Naish 85c]

L. Naish, "All Solutions Predicates In PROLOG", *Proceedings of IEEE Symposium on Logic Programming*, Boston, 1985. Also Technical Report 84/4, Department of Computer Science, University of Melbourne.

[Naish 85d]

L. Naish, "PROLOG Control Rules", *Proceedings of IJCAI*, Los Angeles, 1985. Shortened version of Technical Report 84/13, Department of Computer Science, University of Melbourne.

[Naish 86a]

L. Naish, "Negation and Quantifiers in NU-Prolog", *Proceedings of 3rd International Conference on Logic Programming*, London, 1986. Also Technical Report 85/13, Department of Computer Science, University of Melbourne.

[Naish 86b]

L. Naish, J.A. Thom and K. Ramamohanarao, "Concurrent Database Updates in Prolog", Technical Report 86/12, Department of Computer Science, University of Melbourne, 1986, in preparation.

[Pereira 79]

L. M. Pereira and A. Porto, "Intelligent Backtracking and Sidetracking in Horn Clause Programs: The Theory", Research Report CIUNL No. 2, Departemento de Informatica, Universidade Nova de Lisboa, Portugal, 1979.

[Pereira 81]

L. M. Pereira and A. Porto, "All Solutions", *Logic Programming Newsletter No. 2*, Autumn, 1981.

[Porto 82]

A. Porto, "EPILOG: A Language for Extended Programming in Logic", *Proceedings of the First International Logic Programming Conference*, Marseille, France, September, 1982, 31-37.

[Porto 84]

A. Porto, "Two-Level Prolog", *International Conference On Fifth Generation Computer Systems*, November 1984.

[Ramamohanarao 86]

K. Ramamohanarao and J.A. Shepherd, "A Superimposed Codeword Indexing Scheme for Very Large Prolog Databases", *Proceedings of 3rd International Conference on Logic Programming*, London, 1986. Also Technical Report 85/17, Department of Computer Science, University of Melbourne.

[Reddy 85]

U. S. Reddy, "On the Relationship between Logic and Functional Languages", in *Functional and Logic Programming*, D. DeGroot and G. Lindstrom (editor), Prentice-Hall, 1985.

[Reiter 78]

R. Reiter, "On Closed World Databases", in *Logic and Databases*, H. Gallaire and J. Minker (editor), Plenum Press, 1978, 55-76. Also in Readings in Artificial Intelligence, edited by Webber and Nilsson, published by Tioga, 1981.

[Sagiv 84]

Y. Sagiv and J. D. Ullman, "Complexity of a Top-Down Capture Rule", Technical Report STAN-CS-84-1009, Department of Computer Science, Stanford University, July, 1984.

[Sakai 83]

K. Sakai and T. Miyachi, "Incorporating Naive Negation into Prolog", Technical Report TR-0028, ICOT – Institute for New Generation Computer Technology, Tokyo, Japan, 1983.

[Sato 84]

T. Sato and H. Tamaki, "Transformational Logic Program Synthesis", *International Conference On Fifth Generation Computer Systems*, November 1984.

[Schultz 84]

J. W. Schultz, "The Use Of First-order Predicate Calculus As A Logic Programming System", M.Sc Thesis, Department Of Computer Science, University Of Melbourne, 1984.

[Shapiro 83a]

E. Y. Shapiro, "A Subset of Concurrent Prolog and Its Interpreter", Technical Report TR-003, ICOT – Institute for New Generation Computer Technology, Tokyo, Japan, January, 1983.

[Shapiro 83b]

E. Y. Shapiro and A. Takeuchi, "Object Oriented Programming in Concurrent Prolog", *New Generation Computing 1* (1983), Springer Verlag. Also ICOT Technical Report.

[Shoham 84]

Y. Shoham and D. V. McDermott, "Directed Relations And The Inversion Of Prolog Programs", *International Conference On Fifth Generation Computer Systems*, November 1984.

[Sickel 79]

S. Sickel, "Invertibility of Logic Programs", *Proceedings of the 4th Workshop on Automated Deduction*, 1979.

[Stabler 83]

E. P. Stabler and E. W. Elcock, "Knowledge Representation in an Efficient Deductive Inference System", *Proceedings of Workshop on Logic Programming*, Algarve, Portugal, 1983.

[Tamaki 84]

H. Tamaki and T. Sato, "Unfold/Fold Transformation of Logic Programs", *Proceedings of the Second International Logic Programming Conference*, Uppsala University, Uppsala, Sweden, July, 1984, 127-138.

[Thom 86]

J.A. Thom, K. Ramamohanarao and L. Naish, "A Superjoin Algorithm for Deductive Databases", *Proceedings of 12th International Conference on Very Large Databases*, Kyoto, Japan, 1986. Also Technical Report 86/1, Department of Computer Science, University of Melbourne.

[Ullman 84]

J. D. Ullman, "Implementation of Logical Query Languages for Databases", Technical Report STAN-CS-84-1000, Stanford University, 1984.

[Ullman 85]

J. D. Ullman and A. Van Gelder, "Testing Applicability of Top Down Capture Rules", Technical Report, Stanford University, 1985.

[Warren 79]

D. H. D. Warren, "Coroutining Facilities for Prolog, Implemented in PROLOG", DAI Research Paper, Department of Artificial Intelligence, University of Edinburgh, 1979.

[Warren 81]

D. H. D. Warren, "Efficient Processing of Interactive Relational Database Queries Expressed in Logic", *Proceedings Seventh International Conference on Very Large Data Bases*, Cannes, France, 1981, 272-281.

[Warren 82]

D. H. D. Warren, "Higher-Order Extensions to Prolog: Are They Needed ?", *Machine Intelligence*, 1982.

[Wolfram 84]

D. A. Wolfram, M. J. Maher and J. L. Lassez, "A Unified Treatment of Resolution Strategies for Logic Programs", *Proceedings of the 2nd International Logic Programming Conference*, Sweden, July, 1984. Also Technical Report 83/12, Dept. of Computer Science, University of Melbourne.

APPENDIX 1 – THE MU-PROLOG REFERENCE MANUAL

MU-PROLOG 3.2db REFERENCE MANUAL

Lee Naish
Melbourne University
July 1985

Herein is a description of the facilities of version 3.2db of the MU-PROLOG interpreter, including the external database facilities. This is a reference manual only, not a guide to writing PROLOG programs.

1. INTRODUCTION

MU-PROLOG is (almost) upward compatible with DEC-10 PROLOG, C-PROLOG and (PDP-11) UNIX PROLOG. The syntax and built-in predicates are therefore very similar. A small number of DEC-10 predicates are not available and some have slightly different effects. There are also some MU-PROLOG predicates which are not defined in DEC-10 PROLOG. However most DEC-10 programs should run with few, if any, alterations.

However, MU-PROLOG is not intended to be a UNIX PROLOG look-alike. MU-PROLOG programs should be written in a more declarative style. The non-logical "predicates" such as cut (!), \=, not and var are rarely needed and should be avoided. Instead, the soundly implemented not (~), not equals (~=) and if-then-else should be used and wait declarations should be added where they can increase efficiency.

2. USING MU-PROLOG

To use MU-PROLOG type the shell command "prolog" (this is dependent on the installation). The interpreter will print a short message followed by a prompt. You are now at the top level of the interpreter and if you type PROLOG commands they will be executed. For example, if you type "[myfile]." then the file myfile in your current directory will be consulted (loaded). If you then type "ls." the program will be listed. Commands are PROLOG terms terminated by a full stop and a carriage return.

After you type a goal without variables the top level will print yes or no (depending on whether the goal succeeded or failed). If a goal with variables succeeds then the bindings of the variables are printed, followed by a question mark prompt. If you want to see the rest of the solutions then type a semicolon followed by a return; otherwise just hit return. It is possible that some subgoals get delayed and are never woken. If this happens then a message indicating how many calls have not been executed is printed. The interpreter has not proved or disproved the goal but it is often indicative of an infinite number of solutions.

Because commands are often repeated, especially during debugging, the system saves the most recent ones you type. Each top level prompt contains a command number. If the command you type is a positive number then the command of that number is repeated. If you type "−1." then the previous command is printed and "−2." means the one before that etc. The h (for history) command lists the saved commands.

An alternative way to run MU-PROLOG is possible if you have a saved state (created by the save predicate) in a file (say savefile). If you type

prolog savefile arg1 arg2 ...

or equivalently (with Berkeley UNIX, at least), just

savefile arg1 arg2 ...

then the state is restored and the arguments may be accessed with the argv predicate. In this mode, no initial message is written. There is a utility available on the system to save PROLOG programs. If you type "plsave f.pl dir", then a save file named f is created in directory dir (the default is the current directory). The program in f.pl should have a procedure called main, with one argument. When the saved file is run, main is called with the command line list (from argv) as the argument. To save space, some of the facilities (the debugging package, for example) are not provided by plsave.

3. BUILT-IN PREDICATES

Here are brief descriptions of the predicates supplied by the interpreter. There are also a number of library predicates which should be used freely, rather than re-inventing the same predicates with different definitions and names. The system also has many predicates with names starting with dollar signs. These are protected from the user but to avoid confusion, you should not start predicate names with dollars.

3.1. Internal Database Predicates

The following predicates are used in accessing and updating the database of clauses stored in main memory.

assert(X)

> Adds clause X (a rule or fact) to the database. It is the same as assertz.

asserta(X)

> Adds X at the start of a procedure.

assertz(X)

> Adds X at the end of a procedure.

clause(X,Y)

> There is a clause in the database with head X and body Y. The body of a fact is "true".

clindex(X,Y)

> Y is a procedure head and X is the number of an argument of the procedure. An inverted index is formed for that procedure and argument, so searching for a matching clause can be made much faster. After clindex is called, the procedure cannot be modified.

consult(X)

> The file with name X is consulted. X must be an atom. All clauses and definite clause grammar rules in the file are added to the database and goals are executed. Goals are written in the form "?-goal.".

deny(X,Y)

> Equivalent to retract((X :– Y)).

hidden

> Used in conjunction with hide(X) to hide the implementation of some predicates and make some procedures local to a file.

hide(X)

> X is a procedure name or list of procedure names in the form <procname>(<number of args>). If hide is called at the start of a file being consulted and hidden is called at the end then the effect is to make the procedure(s) local to that file. They cannot be accessed except by other procedures in that file. When hidden procedure names are printed they are followed by an underscore.

lib X

> Reconsults the file named X in the PROLOG library.

libdirectory(X)

> X is the atom whose name is the UNIX directory where the PROLOG library resides.

protect(X)

> X specifies a number of procedures, in the same way as with hide. The procedures are protected, so they can still be called but not listed or altered in any way.

reconsult(X)

> Reads clauses and grammar rules from file X to supersede existing ones (like consult but previous definitions of predicates are retracted).

retract(X)

> The first rule or fact that matches X is removed from the database. On backtracking, the next matching clause is removed.

retractall(X)

> Retracts all clauses whose head matches X.

[file1, file2, ...]

> Consult file1, file2, etc. If "–file1" is used then that file will be reconsulted instead.

3.2. I/O Predicates

These predicates are related to input and output. There are more low level I/O predicates in the UNIX section of this manual.

display(X)

     Write term X on the current output in prefix format. Equivalent to ''writef(X,2'1011)''.

eof(X)

     Equivalent to ''X = (?–end)'' (but more portable).

get(X)

     Reads characters from current input and returns X, the first printing character.

get0(X)

     Returns the next character, X, from the current input. At the end of file it returns 26 ($\wedge$Z).

next(X,Y)

     Changes the standard input to X and the standard output to Y. If X(Y) is ''user'' then the input(output) is not changed. After calling next the new standard input and output are still referred to as ''user''. The old input and output are lost. By default read and write use the standard files but this can be overridden by using see and tell. These should generally be used in preference to next.

nl

     A newline is printed on the current output.

op(X,Y,Z)

     Declares Z, an atom (or list of atoms), to be an operator of type Y and precedence X. The standard operator declarations are nearly all the same as in DEC-10 PROLOG are as listed at the end of this manual.

portraycl(X)

     Write clause X in a suitable format.

portraygoals(X)

     Write goal X in a suitable format.

print(X)

     Print X on the current output. If the user has defined a predicate called ''portray'', with one argument, then this is called. If ''portray(X)'' fails then ''write(X)'' is called.

printf(X,Y)

     List Y is printed with format X. Y is a list of strings, constants and integers. X is a string specifying the format. Exactly the same conventions are used as with printf in the C language. For strings and constants a %s format is used, %ld for decimal output of integers (integers are cast to longs for portability reasons), %lo for octal, %c for characters (small positive integers in PROLOG). Field widths can be specified in the same way as in C. The types of the elements of Y *must* match the format string.

putatom(X)

> Atom X is printed on the current output.

put(X)

> Character X is written on the current output. X may also be a string.

read(X)

> Read a term terminated by a full stop and a whitespace from the current input. If the term contains variables these are considered distinct from all other variables. At end of file read returns "?–end". X must be a variable. If a syntax error in encountered, a message is printed and read fails.

see(X)

> Switches current input to file X. If X has not already been opened by see then it is, otherwise the old file descriptor is used. After calling see, all calls to read, get, get0 and skip cause X to be read. X must be an atom.

seeing(X)

> X names the current input file.

seen

> Closes the current input file and reverts to the standard input.

skip(X)

> Reads characters from current input until X appears or end of file is reached. If X is a list, then it reads until a member of the list is found.

tab(X)

> Prints X spaces on the current output.

tell(X)

> Switches current output to file X.

telling(X)

> X is the current output file.

told

Closes current output and reverts to standard output.

use_if X

Use_if, use_else and use_end allow conditional loading of clauses from files in the same way as #if, #else and #endif in C. The are used as goals (prefixed with ?–). The goal X is called and if it fails, terms are read, from the current input, up to and including the next matching use_else or use_end.

use_else

Use_else reads terms up to and including the next matching use_end.

use_end

Succeeds (does nothing).

wflags(X)

If X is an integer, the write flags are set to X. If X is a variable, it is bound to the current value of the write flags. Write interprets the value as a bit string. If the 1 bit is set, terms are written in prefix format. If the 2 bit is set, names containing non-alphanumeric characters are quoted. If the 4 bit is set, lists of integers between 32 and 126 are written as strings. If the 8 bit is set, level numbers are written after variables, to distinguish between different variables with the same name. If the 16 bit is set, lists are written with the dot notation, instead of brackets. If the 32 bit is set, non-alphanumeric constants are parenthesised. The write flags are initially set to 2'01100.

write(X)

Writes term X on current output, taking into consideration current operator declarations and write flags. Write is currently written recursively, so for deeply nested terms some systems may have problems with the stack size.

writef(X,Y)

Write term X using flags Y, rather than the current write flags.

writeln(X)

The same as "write(X), nl".

3.3. Interactive Predicates

These predicates are usually called from the top level of the interpreter, or used for debugging, rather than being part of programs.

abort

    Aborts execution of the current goal and reverts to top level.

backtrace(X)

    Write the X most recent ancestors.

backtrace

    Write the 10 most recent ancestors.

break

    Causes a new invocation of the top-level interpreter. When this has finished, the previous computation is resumed.

debugging

    Lists all current spypoints.

h

    Print a history of the top level commands that have been saved.

ls

    Write all predicate definitions (except hidden and protected ones).

listing

    Write all predicate definitions (except hidden and protected ones).

ls X

    Write all definitions of predicates named X (except hidden and protected ones). X may be a list of predicate names.

listing X

    Write all definitions of predicates named X (except hidden and protected ones). X may be a list of predicate names.

nodebug

    Removes all spypoints. See "spy".

nospy X

    Removes any spypoints on procedure(s) X.

notrace

>Equivalent to trace(0).

restore(X)

>Restores the prolog state saved in file X. If X is not a compatible save file, restore fails. No files (other than the standard ones) should be open when restore is called.

save(X)

>Saves a copy of the current prolog state in file X. X is made an executable file which, when run or used as the first argument to prolog, restores the state and continues as if the save had just succeeded. No files (other than the standard ones) should be open when save is called.

spy X

>Places a spypoint on procedure(s) X. X is a procedure name or list of procedure names in the form <procname> or <procname>(<number of args>). When a procedure with a spypoint is called a message is printed and the user is able to trace and control the execution.

trace(X)

>Turns universal tracing on/off. X is an integer interpreted as a bit string. If the least significant bit (1) is one then each time the interpreter tries to match a call with a procedure head, a message is printed. The second bit (2) causes messages when backtracking occurs. The third bit (4) causes messages when a calls delay. The fourth bit (8) causes messages when delayed calls are woken. Some system predicates turn tracing off.

trace

>Equivalent to "trace(2'1111)".

3.4. Arithmetic Predicates

The following predicates deal with integers or integer expressions. Integer expressions may contain integers, variables bound to integer expressions, strings of length one and arithmetic operators. The allowable binary operators are +, −, *, /, mod, ∧ (bitwise and), \/ (bitwise or), ∧ (exclusive or), << (shift left), >> (shift right), and (logical and), or (logical or) and the relational operators <, =<, >, >=, =:= and =\=. The valid unary operators are − and \ (bitwise not). Logical expressions evaluate to one (true) or zero (false). All predicates which use integer expressions delay until all variables in the expression(s) are bound.

maxint(X)

>X is the largest integer possible in the system. The smallest is $-X - 1$.

X < Y

    Integer expression X is evaluates to less than integer expression Y.

X =< Y

    Integer expression X is less than or equal to expression Y.

X > Y

    Integer expression X is greater than expression Y.

X >= Y

    Integer expression X is greater than or equal to expression Y.

X =:= Y

    Integer expressions X and Y are equal.

X =\= Y

    Integer expressions X and Y are not equal.

X and Y

    Integer expressions X and Y are both non-zero.

X or Y

    Integer expressions X, Y or both are non-zero.

X is Y

    Integer expression Y evaluates to X (a variable or integer). Remember that it delays if Y contains an unbound variable so it can only be used "in one direction", unlike plus.

plus(X,Y,Z)

    X + Y = Z. If at least two arguments are variables it will delay. If two are integers then the third will be calculated. If all three are integers it acts solely as a test.

length(X,Y)

    X is a list of length Y. X or Y may be variables. If they are both variables, then the call delays.

3.5. Control and Meta Level Predicates

Those predicates in this section which are non-logical, should be avoided where possible.

ancestor(X,Y)

Y is the Xth ancestor (not including "call", ";" or ",") of the current call.

depth(X)

X is the number of ancestors of the current call.

arg(X,Y,Z)

The Xth argument of term Y is Z (delays if X or Y are variables).

functor(X,Y,Z)

X is a term whose functor is Y and arity Z. Delays if X and either Y or Z are variables.

name(X,Y)

Y is the list of characters in the name of atom X. If X and Y are variables, it delays.

atom(X)

X is an atom (non-logical). If X is currently a variable it fails.

atomic(X)

X is an atom or integer (non-logical).

int(X)

X is an integer. If X is currently a variable it delays.

integer(X)

X is an integer (non-logical). If X is currently a variable it fails.

var(X)

X is currently a variable (non-logical).

nonvar(X)

X is not currently a variable (non-logical).

not X

If X succeeds then not X fails and if X fails then not X succeeds. The result is suspect if X succeeds and binds any variables (non-logical – use ~ instead).

~X

Sound implementation of negation as failure. If X contains variables then it delays, otherwise if X succeeds then ~X fails and if X fails then ~X succeeds.

occurs(X,Y)

Term Y contains a subterm X. X must be a variable, an atom or an integer (non-logical).

error(X)

Called when an error occurs (see section 5 of this manual).

errhandler(X)

Called by "error" if the user-defined procedure "traperror(X,Y,Z)" fails (see section 5).

repeat

Always succeeds, even on backtracking.

true

Succeeds. On backtracking it fails.

fail

Always fails.

wait X

X is a procedure head with all its argument either 1 or 0. The corresponding wait declaration is added to the procedure. See section 4 of this manual.

call(X)

The goal represented by the term X.

X

The goal given by the binding of the variable X (meta-variables).

X, Y

X and Y (the bodies of clauses are in this form).

X ; Y

X or Y (use sparingly - use an extra clause instead).

X =.. Y

> Y is a list made up of the functor of X followed by the arguments of X. The call delays if X and Y are insufficiently instantiated. If X is an integer it fails.

X == Y

> Terms X and Y are identical. That is, they can be unified without binding any variables (non-logical).

X \== Y

> X and Y are not identical (non-logical).

X = Y

> X equals Y (X and Y are unified).

X \= Y

> The same as not(X = Y). ie. unsound implementation of not equals.

X ~= Y

> Sound implementation of inequality. If X and Y do not unify it succeeds. If X and Y unify without binding any variables then it fails. If X and Y unify but variables need to be bound then it delays. Underscores in the call are not treated as other variables are. It is assumed that they are universally quantified. For example, X ~= f(_) means for all possible values of _, X does not equal f(_) (so it fails if X equals f(Y), whatever Y is).

if X then Y

> If X contains variables then it delays, otherwise if X succeeds then Y is called. If X fails the goal succeeds.

if X then Y else Z

> If X contains variables then it delays, otherwise if X succeeds then Y is called and if X fails then Z is called.

X -> Y

> Unsound implementation of "if X then Y". It does not delay if X contains variables (non-logical).

X -> Y ; Z

> Unsound implementation of "if X then Y else Z". It does not delay if X contains variables (non-logical).

The cut operation. It succeeds, but on backtracking everything fails up to and including the most recent ancestor which is not ";", "call" or ",". No atoms to the left of the cut are retried and no more clauses in that procedure are tried. It can be used to implement many of the unsafe features of PROLOG (for example, not, \=, var and ==). It should be used as sparingly as possible.

3.6. UNIX-related Predicates

These predicates provide an alternative interface to the file system and other facilities provided by UNIX. The number of predicates in this section is likely to grow with demand.

open(X,Y,Z)

Opens file X (an atom) on channel Y in mode Z. There are currently twenty file channels available. Numbers zero to four are reserved for standard input, standard output, standard error output, current input and current output, respectively. If Y is a variable, then it is bound to the highest free channel. The mode must be 'r' (read), 'w' (write) or 'a' (append).

getc(X,Y)

Y is bound to the value of the next character read on file channel X.

putc(X,Y)

Character Y is written on file channel X.

read(X,Y)

A term Y is read from file channel X.

write(X,Y)

Y is written on file channel X.

write(X,Y,Z)

Y is written on channel X using flags Z.

writeln(X,Y)

Equivalent to "write(X,Y), putc(X,10)".

fprintf(X,Y,Z)

Print list Z on file channel X using format Y.

pipe(X)

>   Creates a pipe named X. X must be an atom. X may then be used with "see", "tell" and "next".

pipe(X,Y)

>   Creates a pipe using file channel X for the input from the pipe and file channel Y for output to it. If X or Y are variables they are bound to the highest free channels.

fork

>   Creates another prolog process, with the same core image. The only difference is that the call to fork in the parent process succeeds but the call in the child process fails. Care must be taken to ensure the two processes do not compete for input from the terminal or other open files.

system(X,Y)

>   Command line X (an atom) is passed to UNIX to execute and Y is then bound to the exit code returned.

argv(X)

>   X is a list of atoms which were the command line arguments typed by the user. The first element of the list will be the name of the save file.

csh

>   Invokes a new copy of the UNIX shell (csh). The prolog process is suspended until the shell process terminates.

sh

>   Invokes a new copy of the UNIX shell (sh).

shell(X)

>   Calls the UNIX shell with the string X as a command line.

more(X)

>   Lists file X using the "more" command.

edit(X)

>   The editor "vi" is used to edit file X. When the editing is completed, the file is reconsulted.

exit(X)

    The prolog process terminates with exit code X (an integer).

getuid(X)

    Binds X to the uid of the user running prolog.

isuser(X)

    Checks the password file for user-name X (X must be a string).

sig(X,Y)

    Used to trap, ignore or set to default, the various UNIX signals. X is the number of a signal as defined in <signal.h>. Y must be zero, to set the signal to the default, one, to ignore the signal, or two, to trap the signal. The most common use is "sig(2,2)" which traps interrupts. This is used at the top level of the interpreter. The library file "signal" gives a more high level interface.

3.7. External Database Predicates

    This section describes the predicates available for the use of external databases to store MU-PROLOG relations. This facility is not available in all versions of the interpreter, and is still under development. For this reason, the predicates here are fairly low-level and are likely to change in the future. Eventually, a more sophisticated system will be available for creating and maintaining databases.

    Database relations behave in the same way as ordinary MU-PROLOG predicates with the following restrictions. The order of the clauses cannot be controlled by the programmer. Concurrent reading and writing is not well defined in PROLOG, and to avoid it with database relations sometimes requires the addition of extra cuts. For example, with "p(X), assert(p(Y))", the call to p(X) is still active (for reading) when assert is called. If cut is called after the call to p(X), the system terminates that database access and so assert can be called.

    A MU-PROLOG database consists of a number of database relations and another file which may contain other (generally small) predicate definitions. For more details, consult the technical report "The MU-PROLOG Deductive Database", by Lee Naish and James Thom.

dbcreate(X).

    An empty database named X (an atom) is created. A UNIX directory of the same name is created and files within it are used to store all information in the database.

dbrules(X,Y).

    Adds the file of rules named Y to database X. The previous rules file is over-written.

createrel(X,Y).

Y specifies a relation to be created in database X. Y must be a list of the form
[relation_name, Br, Bs, Kr, Ks, Ur, Us, Nr, Ns, Nd, Av, "template"]. Relation_name is an
atom specifying the name which will be used to reference the relation from within Prolog
programs. The rest of the elements in the list are numbers specifying various parameters of
the database access method:

Br	-	total number of bits in record descriptors
Bs	-	total number of bits in segment descriptors
Kr	-	number of bits set in record descriptors
Kr	-	number of bits set in segment descriptors
Ur	-	number of bits to use to determine matching records
Us	-	number of bits to use to determine matching segments
Nr	-	number of records per segment
Nr	-	number of segments
Nd	-	number of data files
Av	-	average record length

The total number of records in the file is given by the product of Nr and Ns; if you can
estimate how many records the database will require, it is best to create the file that size to
begin with. The larger the descriptors are, the better will be the retrieval performance, in the
sense of finding less "false matches" (which the Prolog unification routines then has to filter
out); of course, larger descriptors require more storage. The number of bits which are set also
controls the accuracy of hashing but it is expensive to set more bits, and the chance of
generating false segment matches increases as more bits are set and overlayed in the segment
descriptor. The more bits which are used (Us,Ur), the more accurate will be the hash, but it
takes time to test for all these bits. The "template" takes the same form as the relation
would take when used in the program (prefix functional notation), but each element in the
template is a tuple describing properties of the corresponding argument to the relation. It is
envisaged that future versions of the system will have an intelligent interface which can
perform optimization of these parameters using relatively simple information supplied by the
user.

To clarify things a bit, consider the following example of a relation describing an arc in a
graph. Each record in this relation looks something like "connect(arc_id,node1,node2)",
where arc_id is a unique identifying number for arc. We know that there are going to be
around 30000 facts in this database, and each fact will be around 20 characters long, so using
optimization formulas we can derive the following set of paramaters

Br	Bs	Kr	Ks	Ur	Us	Nr	Ns	Nd	Av
47	13934	10	3	10	3	237	96	1	20

Since the most common type of query we will ask on this relation involves finding an arc_id,
given the two node, then we would like to allocate more bits of the codeword from the
second two arguments. Each element in the template has the form "flag:nbits:mask", where
flag tells whether we are ever going to store variables in this field (this allows us to optimize
database access time); the *nbits* field tells relatively how many bits to set for this field (these

values are normalised by the database system); the *mask* field specifies how much weight is to be associated with the field in clustering records within the database.

connect(arc_id, node1, node2)

n:0:0(n:2:2040,n:8:4d9b,n:8:9224)

removerel(X,Y).

Removes the relation named Y from database X. It is not possible to have two relations with the same name in the same database, so the number of arguments is not specified.

dbcons(X).

Database X is consulted. All relations in the database become accessable and the rules file is reconsulted (so this is more like reconsult than consult). Any changes (asserts etc.) to the database relations update the hash file and are therefore permanent. Changes to predicates defined in the rule file, like changes to normal predicates, are lost at the end of the prolog session.

3.8. Dynamic Loading

Some versions of MU-PROLOG allow programs written in C to be compiled then loaded into prolog and linked to a prolog predicate. You need some knowledge of how the interpreter works and, preferably, access to some of the source code. The code you write should be similar to the functions in the interpreter used to implement the built in predicates and normally needs the "types.h" file. Hopefully, this will be documented in a separate report.

Unfortunately, current versions of UNIX do not officially support dynamic loading of object files. Therefore, the implementation may not work completely on all systems. In particular, dynamic loading of object files and saved states may not interact favourably. If a saved state is created after some functions have been dynamically loaded, restoring it may cause trouble. If restoring such a saved state does not seem possible, an attempt is made to exit gracefully. On most systems, restores done at the start of a prolog session should work but after some processing, especially opening files, the chances diminish.

dload(Files, Libs, Entries, Procs).

Files must be a list of atoms which are object file names. Libs must be an atom specifying what libraries are to be used. For example, '-lcurses -lm' causes the cursors and maths libraries to be used. If no libraries (or only the standard C library) are needed, use ' '. Entries must be a list of atoms which are function entry points in the object files. Note that many C compilers prepend an underscore to names, so if your function is called window, the entry point is _window. Procs is a list specifying what prolog procedures the functions are attached to. The length of Procs must be the same as Entries and each element is in the form of a procedure head (only the name and number of arguments is significant).

4. Wait Declarations

Procedures without wait declarations behave as normal PROLOG procedures - calls to them succeed or fail. If wait declarations are added, calls may also delay. This happens when the call unifies with the head of some clause but in doing so, certain of variables in the call are bound. Wait declarations can be used to prevent infinite loops and to enable coroutining between sub-goals, which often increases efficiency.

Wait declarations are most easily added by putting goals in the files containing programs. A typical predicate definition would have a couple of goals to add wait declarations ("?– wait ...") to the clauses for the procedure. The argument to the call to wait should look like the head of one of the clauses with each argument being a one or a zero. A one signifies that the corresponding argument in a call to the procedure may be constructed and a zero means that it may not.

As each argument of a call is being unified with the corresponding argument in a procedure head we check if it is constructed. An argument is constructed if a variable in it is unified with a non-variable in the clause head. If the unification succeeds, the result is a mask of ones and zeros, representing which arguments were and were not constructed. This is then compared with the wait declarations. If there is a wait declaration with ones corresponding to all ones in the mask then we succeed; otherwise we delay.

When a call is delayed the bindings are removed. Thus from a logical point of view nothing has happened. However, the variables that were bound are marked and when any of them are bound by some other call, the delayed call is woken. A call may bind several marked variables and each one may have been marked several times so any number of delayed calls may be woken at the same time. The order of subsequent calls is as if the woken calls were all at the start of the clause that just matched, in the order that they were delayed. For further discussion of the use of wait declarations, see "An Introduction to MU-PROLOG" or "Automating Control for Logic Programs". There is also a preprocessor, lpp, available, which produces reasonable wait declarations for most procedures. It is used as follows:

    lpp < prog > newprog

On non-Berkeley systems, something like the following is needed.

    prolog /usr/lib/prolog/lpp < prog > newprog

5. ERRORS

Whenever an error occurs, procedure error is called with the error code and the call that caused the error as arguments. The call to error in effect replaces the call that caused the error. This allows you to simulate failure, success and replacing the call with another call. When error is called it always prints a message (on standard error) and depending on the error it will do various things.

If the program is almost out of memory then an error is generated, the last ancestors are written and abort is called. If you hit the interrupt key an error is generated. If you hit it again it will get you back to the top level of the interpreter (abort is called). It is an error to call a predicate for which no clauses or wait declarations have ever been added. In such cases, a warning is printed and (in effect) the call fails.

Other errors will cause the error code (and/or some explanation) and the call to be printed, followed by a question mark prompt. The simplest thing to do is to hit interrupt, which generates an abort. If you type a goal it will be executed in place of the call (eg "fail." will cause a failure). If you type a clause then the call is unified with its head and then the body is executed. This can save some typing and allows you to change the call but still use the same variables.

MU-PROLOG also allows users to write their own error handlers, rather than rely on the default one outlined so far. Procedure error is defined in (something like) the following way:

```
error(Ecode, Call) :- traperror(Ecode, Call, X), !, call(X).
error(Ecode, Call) :- errhandler(Ecode, Call).
```

User programs may contain definitions of traperror and other predicates to trap and handle errors, respectively. For example, if you want "is" to fail if it encounters any errors and you want to query the user if an undefined predicate is called, then the following code would do.

```
traperror(_, _ is _, fail).
traperror(enoproc, Call, askabout(Call)).

askabout(Call) :- ...
```

The following error codes are currently used:

eelist	list expected
eeconst	constant expected
eeint	integer expected
eefunctfunctor	expected
eestring	string expected
ee01	one or zero expected
eevar	variable expected
eerwa	r, w or a expected
euint	unexpected integer
eufunct	unexpected functor
euvar	unexpected variable
enoproc	undefined procedure called
eprotect	protection violation
eopen	cant open file
efile	invalid file specification

6. STANDARD OPERATOR DECLARATIONS

?– op(1200, fx, (?–)).	?– op(700, xfx, ==).
?– op(1200, fx, (:–)).	?– op(700, xfx, \==).
?– op(1200, xfx, (:–)).	?– op(700, xfx, =:=).
?– op(1200, xfx, (––>)).	?– op(700, xfx, =\=).
?– op(1170, fx, (if)).	?– op(680, xfy, or).
?– op(1160, xfx, (else)).	?– op(660, xfy, and).
?– op(1150, xfx, (then)).	?– op(630, xfx, <).
?– op(1100, xfy, (–>)).	?– op(630, xfx, >).
?– op(1050, xfy, (;)).	?– op(630, xfx, =<).
?– op(1000, xfy, ',').	?– op(630, xfx, >=).
?– op(900, fy, ls).	?– op(600, xfy, '.').
?– op(900, fy, listing).	?– op(500, yfx, +).
?– op(900, fy, wait).	?– op(500, yfx, –).
?– op(900, fy, ~).	?– op(500, yfx, ∧).
?– op(900, fy, not).	?– op(500, yfx, \/).
?– op(900, fy, \+).	?– op(500, fx, (+)).
?– op(900, fy, nospy).	?– op(500, fx, (–)).
?– op(900, fy, spy).	?– op(500, fx, \).
?– op(900, fy, lib).	?– op(400, yfx, *).
?– op(700, xfx, =).	?– op(400, yfx, /).
?– op(700, xfx, ~=).	?– op(400, yfx, <<).
?– op(700, xfx, \=).	?– op(400, yfx, >>).
?– op(700, xfx, is).	?– op(300, xfx, mod).
?– op(700, xfx, =..).	?– op(200, xfy, '∧').
?– op(1190, fx, (use_if)).	

7. SAMPLE MU-PROLOG SESSION

$ more test.pl

% arg2 is a permutation of the list arg1
perm([ ], [ ]).
perm(A, C.D) :– delete(C, A, E), perm(E, D).

% arg3 is the list arg2 with the element arg1 deleted
delete(A, A.B, B).
delete(A, B.C, B.E) :– delete(A, C, E).

$ prolog

MU-PROLOG Version 3.1

1?– ['test.pl'].   % file names need quotes if they contain . etc.
consulting test.pl
done

yes

2?– delete(X, 1.2.3.[ ], Y).   % delete can be used for deleting list elements

X = 1
Y = [2, 3] ? ;   % (you type ; if you want more solutions)

X = 2
Y = [1, 3] ? ;   % (this is the same as 1.3.[ ])

X = 3
Y = [1, 2] ? ;
no (more) solutions

3?– delete(3, X, 1.2.[ ]).   % and also for inserting

X = [3, 1, 2] ? ;

X = [1, 3, 2] ? ;

X = [1, 2, 3] ? ;
no (more) solutions

4?– perm(1.2.3.[ ], X).   % lets try some permutations

X = [1, 2, 3] ? ;

X = [1, 3, 2] ? ;

X = [2, 1, 3] ?   % thats enough - just hit return

5?– perm(X, 1.2.[ ]).

X = [1, 2] ?   % if we typed ; here we would get into an infinite loop

6?– lib perm.   % this loads the library version of perm
reconsulting /usr/lib/prolog/pllib/perm
done

yes

7?– h.   % list history of commands
1   ['test.pl']
2   delete(X, [1, 2, 3], Y)
3   delete(3, X, [1, 2])
4   perm([1, 2, 3], X)
5   perm(X, [1, 2])
6   lib perm
7   h

yes

8?– 4.   % repeat command 4 (with perm defined differently)
perm([1, 2, 3], X)

X = [1, 2, 3] ? ;

X = [1, 3, 2] ?

9?– 5.   % this version works backwards too
perm(X, [1, 2])

X = [1, 2] ? ;

X = [2, 1] ? ;
no (more) solutions

10?– ls.   % list all predicate definitions

?– wait perm(1, 0).   % this is control information - it can be generated
?– wait perm(0, 1).   % automatically by the genwait library program
perm([ ], [ ]).
perm(A.B, C.D) :–
      delete(C, A.B, E),

perm(E, D).

?– wait delete(1, 0, 1).
?– wait delete(0, 1, 0).
delete(A, A.B, B).
delete(A, B.C.D, B.E) :–
    delete(A, C.D, E).

yes

11?–   % hit end of file char to get out
End of session

APPENDIX 2 – THE MU-PROLOG DEDUCTIVE DATABASE

This technical report gives a fairly accurate description of the database facilities of MU-PROLOG 3.1db. The latest version of the system is implemented rather differently, and has fewer restrictions, as well as being faster. In particular, arbitrary clauses (including variables) may be stored, and there is no restriction on the number of concurrent queries to the database.

THE MU-PROLOG DEDUCTIVE DATABASE

by

Lee Naish and James A. Thom

Technical Report 83/10

Department of Computer Science
The University of Melbourne

Abstract

This paper describes the implementation and an application of a deductive database being developed at the University of Melbourne.

The system is implemented by adding a partial match retrieval system to the MU-PROLOG interpreter.

CR Categories and Subject Descriptors:
    H.2.3 [**Database Management**]: Languages - *query languages*
    I.2.3 [**Artificial Intelligence**]: Deduction and Theorem Proving - *Logic programming*
General Terms
    languages
Additional Key Words and Phrases:
    deductive database, PROLOG, partial match retrieval, UNIX

1. INTRODUCTION

This report describes the MU-PROLOG deductive database facility. The system is still under development and some details of the implementation may be changed. Figure 1 shows the architecture of the MU-PROLOG deductive database. A user is able to access the database via a number of user interfaces. A logic engine (the MU-PROLOG interpreter - Naish 1983a) provides the link between the various user interfaces and the external database containing relations stored in secondary memory. The main components of the system are as follows:

(1)   The MU-PROLOG interpreter.

(2)   The interface between the MU-PROLOG interpreter and the external database.

(3)   The partial match system using recursive linear hashing and descriptors.

One use currently being made of the database, is recording information about all students in the Computer Science Department. This is used as an example. The MU-PROLOG deductive database has some novel features, not present in other systems.

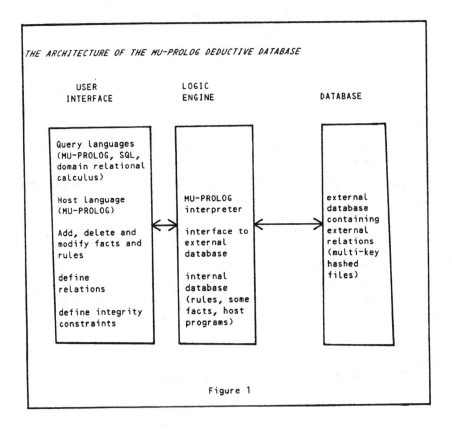

Figure 1

2. DESCRIPTION

2.1. MU-PROLOG facilities

The highest level concept provided by the database facility of MU-PROLOG is that of databases. A database is made up of a number of relations, consisting of ground unit clauses stored on disc, and a set of procedures, containing facts and/or rules, which are read into main memory. If a PROLOG program changes some of the procedures, only the copies in main memory are affected. Changes only last for one session of prolog. However, if a relation is updated, files are altered, so the changes are permanent. MU-PROLOG has the following commands to create, alter and access databases.

dbcreate(db).

> Creates a database named "db". A directory named "db" is created and within this, all the database files will be stored.

dbrules(db, rules_file).

> Adds a file of rules (and/or facts) to the database "db". Any existing procedures are replaced by the ones in file "rules_file". When "dbcons" is called, these procedures are loaded into memory. It is a wise to keep a copy of the file, so if the rules need to be changed, it can be edited and "dbrules" can be called again.

createrel(db, relation_spec).

> Adds a relation to the database "db". The name of the relation and the number of arguments must be specified, along with information from which the most efficient form of indexing is calculated.

removerel(db, relation_spec).

> Removes a relation.

dbcons(db).

> Database "db" is consulted. All the procedures are read in and the relations are made accessible. Previous definitions of the procedures and relations are removed, so it is similar to "reconsult" in normal MU-PROLOG.

On a slightly lower level, we have procedures and relations. Procedures are just ordinary MU-PROLOG procedures. The relations are also PROLOG procedures but they are slightly restricted. Only ground unit clauses are allowed and the order of the facts cannot be controlled by the programmer. There is no general way to assert a fact at the start of a relation, for example. These differences aside, relations can be accessed and modified in the same way as procedures stored in main memory.

At the level of calls to access relations, the only differences are at the implementation level, which is transparent to the user. There are three basic actions that require access: calling a relation directly, asserting a fact into it and retracting a fact from it. Calls to the built-in predicate "clause" can be implemented by calling the relation, since it only contains facts. Similarly, a version of the "retract" predicate which is retried on backtracking is implemented by calling the relation and then calling a procedure to retract a single fact.

The MU-PROLOG system needs to know what relations currently exist (and in what databases they are stored). Each database has a file listing its contents, so "dbcons" can easily keep track of all the relations. The three database access methods are also needed and are provided by the *database interface*. The implementation is discussed in the next section but first we give a more detailed account of what is required.

(1) *Calls.*

Calls to relations are partial match queries to the database. The MU-PROLOG system supplies the interface with a query and the name of the database in which the relation is stored. The interface must then query the database and make the list of answers available to prolog. These answers are used one at a time (as prolog backtracks) and between getting successive answers to one query, several other database accesses may be made. When the last answer is returned the query has been completed. Due to the cut operation in PROLOG, it is possible that the last answer will never be requested. In this case, prolog can tell the interface to prematurely terminate that query.

(2) *Asserts.*

To assert into a relation, prolog must provide the interface with a ground fact and a database name. No information is returned but the fact should actually be asserted, before the prolog can continue. In some cases it does not matter if the asserts are done asynchronously and queued. This would save prolog from waiting and could be provided as an option.

(3) *Retracts.*

Here prolog provides the interface with a database name and a fact which may contain variables. The interface returns the ground fact which it actually retracted or indicates in some way that there were no matches.

As well as the facilities to access relations on disc, MU-PROLOG has additional control and negation facilities, which are particularly important in a system where the users are not expected to be experts. In a typical PROLOG system, the way in which a query is expressed has a marked effect on efficiency and may also affect correctness, if negation is involved. The implementation of negation in MU-PROLOG ensures correctness and the control facilities can be used to improve efficiency (Naish 1982). A further control facility is planned, which is particularly useful for database applications (Naish 1983b).

2.2. Interface to database

The interface between MU-PROLOG and the database creates a number of partial match processes. Each (concurrent) query, assert or retract uses a separate process. Each partial match process is dedicated to a particular relation and can receive a series of requests which it processes one at a time.

The input to each each partial match process is referred to as the *request stream* and carries any of these requests (in a suitably coded form):

(1)   A *Query* of the form relation(t_1,...,t_n) where the t_i are terms.

(2)   An *Assertion* of the form assert(relation(t_1,...,t_n)) where the t_i are ground terms.

(3)   A *Retraction* of the form retract(relation(t_1,...,t_n)) where the t_i are terms.

The output is referred to as the *answer stream* and carries answers to queries and retractions and confirmation of assertions back to MU-PROLOG – see Figure 2.

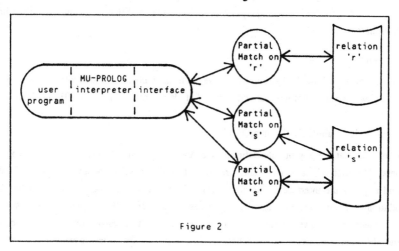

Figure 2

In setting up each query (or assert or retract) the MU-PROLOG interpreter calls the interface to the partial match system. The parameters to this call include:
– the database name
– a term
– the type of request (assert, retract or query)

The interface keeps track of all the partial match processes, including what state they are in. Each partial match process is either *active* (in the middle of processing a query) or *passive*. The interface uses the database and relation names to set up a new process when it is unable to find an existing passive process with the same relation identifier.

When the MU-PROLOG interpreter sets up a query it is able to read the answer to the request from the answer stream. Upon reading an *end-of-answer* from the answer stream the interpreter calls the interface, so that the interface can change the state of that particular process from active to passive. Also, if the interpreter backtracks over a query without reading the end-of-answer, it must then call the interface to abort that process.

At present the query and answer streams are implemented using UNIX pipes. There is a limit to the number of pipes that can be connected to a process and this limits the number of partial match processes possible (currently seven). Thus it is sometimes necessary to kill a passive process belonging to one relation to answer a request to another relation. This does limit the use of some programs, particularly those with recursive rules which access database relations, such as the following.

    ancestor(X, Y) :- parent(X, Y).
    ancestor(X, Y) :- parent(Z, Y), ancestor(X, Z).

If the parent relation is stored in a database on disc, the number of recursive calls is limited by the maximum number of partial match processes. It is possible to increase the limit by altering an internal constant within the operating system, or by using a different method of inter-process communication.

2.3. An Example

As an example of how the system works, we shall use a query to a student database. Suppose we want to know the enrolment number and name of students enrolled in units 101 and 102:

    ← unit(E, 101), unit(E, 102), name(E, N).

We assume that the appropriate definitions of the "unit" and "name" relations are stored in the database. The first call is to the "unit" relation. MU-PROLOG recognises that it is a database relation and requests the interface to initiate a query. The interface has no passive processes for the "unit" relation so it must set up a new active process, which we will call process one; also it must set up the request and answer streams to process one. It then sends the query down the request stream and the interpreter waits for the first answer to arrive from the answer stream. We will represent this situation as follows:

    ← process1(unit(E, 101)), unit(E, 102), name(E, N).   (1)

Suppose now, the first answer received is "unit(772217, 101)". This is unified with the call, binding E to 772217:

    ← unit(772217, 102), name(772217, N).

Now "unit" is called again and the interface sets up another active process (process two) and sends the query to it:

    ← process2(unit(772217, 102)), name(772217, N).

If there are no matches to the call, then the first thing sent down the answer stream is end-of-answer. Process two is then set to "passive" and the call fails. MU-PROLOG backtracks over this call to (1), removing the binding of E. The second answer to the first query is now read from the answer stream of process one. Because process one was producing answers in parallel (reading ahead), there is probably no waiting needed. Suppose the answer returned is "unit(772304, 101)", so E is bound to 772304:

    ← unit(772304, 102), name(772304, N).

This time, when the interface is asked to call "unit", there is already a passive process (process two) available for the "unit" relation. This is set to active and the query is sent down the request stream:

    ← process2(unit(772304, 102)), name(772304, N).

Suppose, this time, the call succeeds:

    ← name(772304, N).

Now a third and final active process (process three) will be created, to access relation "name" and the query will be sent to it:

    ← process3(name(772304, N)).

When the answer to this query (say, "name(772304, smith)") is read from the stream, N is bound to 'smith' and the query succeeds. If further solutions are required, prolog backtracks, undoing bindings but retaining the processes, as before. Because process was executing in parallel, there is little or no delay before the execution proceeds forwards again, re-using the same processes. If the user does not need all solutions, then the three queries must be aborted.

2.4. Partial Match Retrieval System

The database stores each relation in a separate file (actually files) and accesses the tuples in that relation by *partial match retrieval using recursive linear hashing and descriptors*. This access scheme is a combination of the schemes described by Ramamohanarao, Lloyd and Thom (1983), Ramamohanarao, and Sacks-Davis (1983a), and Ramamohanarao, and Sacks-Davis (1983b).

Recursive linear hashing is an extension of a method originally proposed by Litwin (1980) for a hashing technique for files which grow and shrink dynamically. Recursive linear hashing eliminates the need for conventional overflow records. If a record does not fit into the primary storage area then it is stored in a secondary linear hashed file (and so forth). This technique is described in Ramamohanarao, and Sacks-Davis (1983a).

By constructing the hashing function in the way described in Ramamohanarao, and Sacks-Davis (1983b) it is possible to use this scheme to efficiently access files via multi-key combinations.

Finally descriptors are added to this scheme to reduce the number of pages in the main file which actually have to be examined. Descriptors are used for each page in each linear hashed file. The use of descriptors to improve the performance of partial match schemes is described in Ramamohanarao, Lloyd and Thom (1983).

3. AN APPLICATION – STUDENT DATABASE

Since the begining of 1983, the MU-PROLOG deductive database has been used to store information on all the students in the Computer Science Department at The University of Melbourne. Enrolment information stored in the database was used for creating student accounts and allocating recources to them.

3.1. Relations

The following are some relations in the student database:

```
relation(freeuid(Uid)).
relation(stud_unit(Enrol,Unit)).
relation(student(Enrol,Sname,Gnames,Uname,Uid,CrsA,CrsB,Year,Attend)).
relation(mark(Uname,Unit,Project,Mark)).
```

3.2. Application Programs

The following are some application programs which access the database, two of these (info and eddb) are listed in the appendix.

mkdb

Make the database from the file supplied by the University administration.

eddb student

Edit the entry in the database for the particular student.

info student

Print information about a particular student or students.

extract

Extract information from the database.

Two predicates, "priv" and "signal", provide access to Unix system calls. These are necessary to allow students to access their own entry in the database but not invade the privacy of others. The implications of deductive and similar databases for personal privacy are discussed in Thom and Thorne (1983).

4. RELATED WORK

A substantial amount of work has been done on assimilating logic programming and databases. Gallaire (1983) has proposed a categorization of such systems, from logic programming with database facilities to databases with deductive facilities. The MU-PROLOG system lies near the logic programming end of the scale, either PROLOG+ or PROLOG DB, in Gallaire's terminology. These systems, such as Bruynooghe (1981) and Chomicki and Grundzinski (1983), generally have similar facilities available to the PROLOG programmer.

The unique aspects of the MU-PROLOG system are the implementation of the database interface, the file structure and the facilities for negation and control. The interface allows asynchronous reading ahead and is very easy to modify so, for example, another file access method could be used. The reading ahead and sophisticated hashing scheme should be the basis of and efficient database system. The control and negation offer extra user convenience.

ACKNOWLEDGEMENT

The authors wish to thank John Lloyd for instigating this project and continuing to spur us on.

APPENDIX

The appendix contains listings of the ".con" and ".rules" files from the student database and listings of two programs "info.pl" and "eddb.pl".

".con"

```
relation(freeuid(Uid)).
relation(stud_unit(Enrol,Unit)).
relation(student(Enrol,Sname,Gnames,Uname,Uid,CrsA,CrsB,Year,Attend)).
relation(mark(Uname,Unit,Project,Mark)).
```

".rules"

```
priv(student) :- privilege(1).
priv(tutor) :- privilege(2).
priv(super_tute) :- privilege(3).

uid(Enrol,Uid) :- student(Enrol,_,_,_,Uid,_,_,_,_).
unam(Enrol,Unam) :- student(Enrol,_,_,Unam,_,_,_,_,_).

enstud(E,X) :- student(E,S,G,U,I,A,B,Y,T),X = student(E,S,G,U,I,A,B,Y,T).
usrstud(U,X) :- student(E,S,G,U,I,A,B,Y,T),X = student(E,S,G,U,I,A,B,Y,T).
idstud(I,X) :- student(E,S,G,U,I,A,B,Y,T),X = student(E,S,G,U,I,A,B,Y,T).

traperror(Err, Call, err(Err, Call)).

err(Err, Call) :- printf("Error %s, call = ", [Err]),
            writeln(Call),
            exit(1).

course(0,"Null").
course(104,"BA(Hons)").
course(105,"BA").
course(205,"BCom").
course(355,"BE").
course(365,"BE(Agr)").
```

```
course(375,"BE(Chem)").
course(395,"BE(Elect)").
course(415,"BE(Mech)").
course(445,"BSurv").
course(465,"BAppSc").
course(505,"LLB").
course(555,"MBBS").
course(655,"BMus").
course(754,"BSc(Hons)").
course(755,"BSc").
course(756,"DipComp").
course(759,"AddSubjSc").
course(765,"BScEd").
course(785,"BSc(Optom)").
course(X,Y) :- str_int(Y,X).
```

"info.pl"

```
main(_.'-d'.Db.Users) :-
                !,
                dbcons(Db),
                main(info.Users).
main(_.User1.Users) :-
                priv(super_tute),
                info(User1.Users),
                exit(0).
main(_._._) :-
                writeln('Bad luck'),
                exit(1).
main(_.[]) :-
                getuid(Uid),
                prinfo(En,Uname, Uid),
                exit(0).
main(_) :-
                /* never happens */
                writeln('Usage: info [-d db] [user ...]'),
                exit(1).
```

```
info([ ]).
info(User.R) :-
            int_const(En, User),
            (
                    prinfo(En,Uname, Uid),
                    fail

            ;

                    info(R)
            ).
info(User.R) :-
            const_str(User, Uname),
            (
                    prinfo(En,Uname, Uid),
                    fail

            ;

                    info(R)
            ).


prinfo(En,Uname, Uid) :-
            student(En, Sname, Gnames, Uname, Uid, CrsA, CrsB, Year, Att),
            printf("User:%s(%d)%c",[Uname,Uid,10]),
            printf("Enrolment number:%d%c%s %s%c",
                    [En, 10, Gnames, Sname, 10]),
            (if CrsB = 0 then
                    course(CrsA,A),
                    printf("Course: %s%c", [A, 10])
            else
                    course(CrsA,A),
                    course(CrsB,B),
                    printf("Primary course: %s%c", [A, 10]),
                    printf("Secondary course: %s%c", [B, 10])
            ),
            printf("Year: %d%c", [Year, 10]),
            printf("Attendance Type: %s%c", [Att, 10]),
            printf("Units:", []),
            prunit(En),
            !.
prinfo(_,_,_) :-
            printf("NOT IN DATABASE",[]),
            nl,
            nl.
```

```
prunit(En) :-
                stud_unit(En, Unit),
                printf(" %d",[Unit]),
                fail.
prunit(_) :-
                nl,
                nl.


?-lib convert.
?-dbcons('/usr/adm/studdb').
```

"eddb.pl"

```
main(_.User.[]) :-
        priv(super_tute),
        eddb(User),
        exit(0).
main(_._.[]) :-
        writeln('Get Stuffed'),
        exit(1).
main(_) :-
        writeln('Usage: eddb user'),
        exit(1).


eddb(User) :-
        int_const(En, User),
        newinfo(En,Uname).
eddb(User) :-
        const_str(User, Uname),
        newinfo(En,Uname).


newinfo(En,Uname) :-
        student(En, Sname, Gnames, Uname, Uid, CrsA, CrsB, Year, Att),
        printf("User: %s(%d)%c",[Uname,Uid,10]),
        printf("Enrolment number:%d%c", [En, 10]),
        newstr("Surname", Sname, New_Sname,sname(New_Sname),
                "UPPER CASE ONLY"),
        newstr("Given names", Gnames, New_Gnames,gnames(New_Gnames),
```

```
                        "First Letters Upper Case Only"),
          newint("Primary course", CrsA, New_CrsA, course(New_CrsA),
                        "Course number expected"),
          newint("Secondary course", CrsB, New_CrsB, course(New_CrsB),
                        "Course number expected"),
          newint("Year", Year, New_Year, year(New_Year),[ ]),
          newconst("Attendance Type", Att, New_Att, attend(New_Att),
                        "f/t, p/t, n/a or raaf"),
          newunits(En),
          retract(student(En, Sname, Gnames, Uname, Uid, CrsA, CrsB, Year, Att)),
          assert(student(En, New_Sname, New_Gnames, Uname, Uid,
                        New_CrsA, New_CrsB, New_Year, New_Att)),
          !.
newinfo(En,Uname) :-
          nonvar(En),
          newstr("Surname", [ ], Sname, sname(Sname), "UPPER CASE ONLY"),
          newstr("Given names", [ ], Gnames, gnames(Gnames),
                        "First Letters Upper Case Only"),
          mkunam(Sname,Gnames,Uname),
          printf("User: %s%c",[Uname,10]),
          newint("Primary course", [ ], CrsA, course(CrsA),
                        "Course number expected"),
          newint("Secondary course", [ ], CrsB, course(CrsB),
                        "Course number expected"),
          newint("Year", [ ], Year, year(Year),[ ]),
          newconst("Attendance Type", [ ], Att, attend(Att),
                        "f/t, p/t, n/a or raaf"),
          newunits(En),
          retract(freeuid(Uid)),
          assert(student(En, Sname, Gnames, Uname, Uid, CrsA, CrsB, Year, Att)).
newinfo(En,Uname) :-
          writeln('No such user'),
          exit(1).


newunits(En) :-
          all(X, stud_unit(En, X), Ucurru),
          sort(Ucurru, Curru),
          chunits(Curru, Newu),
          signal(sigint,sig_ign),
          signal(sigquit,sig_ign),
          signal(sighup,sig_ign),
```

```prolog
            signal(sigtstp,sig_ign),
            Newu ~= Curru,
            retractall(stud_unit(En, _)),
            member(U, Newu),
            assert(stud_unit(En, U)),
            fail.
newunits(_).

chunits(Curru, Newu) :-
            writeln('Current units:'),
            delunits(Curru, Remu),
            addunits(Extrau),
            append(Remu, Extrau, Newu).


delunits([ ], [ ]).
delunits(U.R, X) :-
            printf("      Keep %d", [U]),
            newstr(" ", "y", Ans, (Ans = "y" ; Ans = "n"), "y or n"),
            (
                  Ans = "y",
                  X = U.Y,
                  delunits(R, Y)

            ;

                  Ans ~= "y",
                  delunits(R, X)

            ).


addunits(X) :-
            write('Additional unit: '),
            getline(L),
            (
                  str_int(L, U),
                  (
                        unit(U),
                        X = U.R,
                        addunits(R)

                  ;

                        writeln('Not a valid unit'),
                        addunits(X)

                  )

            ;
```

```
                X = []
        ),
        !.


year(X) :-
                X > 0,
                X < 9.
course(X) :-
                X >= 0,
                X < 1000.
unit(X) :-                      /* this (and course) should be extended */
                X > 99,
                X < 1000.
attend('f/t').
attend('p/t').
attend('n/a').
attend(raaf).

sname([ ]).
sname(C.N) :-
                "A" =< C,
                C =< "Z",
                sname(N).
sname(C.N) :-
                member(C, "'- ''),
                sname(N).

gnames([ ]).
gnames(C.N) :-
                "A" =< C,
                C =< "Z",
                names(N).

names([ ]).
names(C.N) :-
                "a" =< C,
                C =< "z",
                names(N).
names(C.N) :-
                member(C, "'-''),
```

```
                    names(N).
names(C.N) :-
                C is " ",
                gnames(N).
/* output old value (if any) and input new (CR for no change) */


newint(Mess, Curr, New, Test, Emess) :-
      repeat,
      (if Curr ~= [ ] then
              printf("%s <%d>: ", [Mess, Curr])
      else
              printf("%s: ", [Mess])
      ),
      getline(Line),
      (
              Line = [ ],
              Curr ~= [ ],
              New = Curr

      ;
              Line ~= [ ],
              str_int(Line,New),
              Test

      ;
              Emess ~= [ ],
              printf("%s%c", [Emess, 10]),
              fail
      ),
      !.


newconst(Mess, Curr, New, Test, Emess) :-
      repeat,
      (if Curr ~= [ ] then
              printf("%s <%s>: ", [Mess, Curr])
      else
              printf("%s: ", [Mess])
      ),
      getline(Line),
      (
              Line = [ ],
              Curr ~= [ ],
              New = Curr
```

```
            ;
                    Line ~= [],
                    const_str(New,Line),
                    Test
            ;
                    Emess ~= [],
                    printf("%s%c", [Emess, 10]),
                    fail
            ),
            !.


newstr(Mess, Curr, New, Test, Emess) :-
        repeat,
        (if Curr ~= [ ] then
                printf("%s <%s>: ", [Mess, Curr])
        else
                printf("%s: ", [Mess])
        ),
        getline(Line),
        (
                Line = [ ],
                New = Curr
        ;
                Line ~= [ ],
                Line = New,
                Test
        ;
                Emess ~= [ ],
                printf("%s%c", [Emess, 10]),
                fail
        ),
        !.


getline(X) :-
        get0(Y),
        (
                Y = 10,
                X = []
        ;
                Y ~= 10,
                X = Y.Z,
```

```
          getline(Z)
     ).


sort([ ], [ ]).
sort(A.B, C.D) :–
          sort(B, E),
          insert(A, E, C.D).


insert(A, [ ], A.[ ]).
insert(A, B.C, A.B.C) :–
          A =< B.
insert(A, B.C, B.D) :–
          A > B,
          insert(A, C, D).


?–[–'mkunam.con'].
?–lib convert.
?–lib signal.
?–dbcons('/usr/adm/studdb').
```

REFERENCES FOR APPENDIX 2

Bruynooghe, M. (1981): *PROLOG-C Implementation*, University of Leuven, 1981.

Chomicki and Grundzinski (1983): A Database Support System for PROLOG, *Proceedings, Logic Programming Workshop '83*, Algarve, Portugal, July 1983, pp 290-303.

Gallaire, H. (1983): Logic Databases vs Deductive Databases, *Proceedings, Logic Programming Workshop '83*, Algarve, Portugal, July 1983, pp 608-622.

Naish, L. (1982): *An Introduction to MU-PROLOG*, Technical Report 82/2, (revised July 1983), Department of Computer Science, The University of Melbourne.

Naish, L. (1983a): *MU-PROLOG 3.0 Reference Manual*, Department of Computer Science, The University of Melbourne.

Naish, L. (1983b): *Automatic Generation of Control for Logic Programs*, Technical Report 83/6, Department of Computer Science, The University of Melbourne.

Ramamohanarao, K., Lloyd, J.W. and Thom, J.A. (1983): Partial Match Retrieval Using Hashing and Descriptors, *ACM Trans. on Database Systems*.

Ramamohanarao, K., and Sacks-Davis, R. (1983a): *Recursive Linear Hashing*, Technical Report 83/1, Department of Computing, RMIT.

Ramamohanarao, K., and Sacks-Davis, R. (1983b): *Partial Match Retrieval Using Recursive Linear Hashing.*

Thom, J.A. and Thorne, P.G. (1983): Privacy Legislation and the Right of Access, *Australian Computer Journal,* Vol 15, No 4, pp 145-150.